Palgrave Hate Studies

Series Editors
Neil Chakraborti, School of Criminology, University of Leicester,
Leicester, UK
Barbara Perry, Faculty of Social Science and Humanities, University of
Ontario, Oshawa, Canada

This series builds on recent developments in the broad and interdisciplinary field of hate studies. Palgrave Hate Studies aims to bring together in one series the very best scholars who are conducting hate studies research around the world. Reflecting the range and depth of research and scholarship in this burgeoning area, the series welcomes contributions from established hate studies researchers who have helped to shape the field, as well as new scholars who are building on this tradition and breaking new ground within and outside the existing canon of hate studies research.

Editorial Advisory Board
Tore Bjorgo (Norwegian Institute of International Affairs)
Jon Garland (University of Surrey)
Nathan Hall (University of Portsmouth)
Gail Mason (University of Sydney)
Jack McDevitt (Northeastern University)
Scott Poynting (The University of Auckland)
Mark Walters (University of Sussex)
Thomas Brudholm (University of Copenhagen)

Hannah Mason-Bish

Disability, Gender, Bodies and Boundaries

How Disabled Women Experience Ableist Intrusions

Hannah Mason-Bish
Department of Sociology
and Criminology
Faculty of Social Sciences
University of Sussex
Brighton, UK

ISSN 2947-6364   ISSN 2947-6372 (electronic)
Palgrave Hate Studies
ISBN 978-3-031-85889-5   ISBN 978-3-031-85890-1 (eBook)
https://doi.org/10.1007/978-3-031-85890-1

This Palgrave Macmillan imprint is published by the registered company Springer Nature Switzerland AG
The registered company address is: Gewerbestrasse 11, 6330 Cham, Switzerland

If disposing of this product, please recycle the paper.

For Susie Balderston, rest in power.

PREFACE

Don't put us down like dogs. Please don't vote Tory, don't walk past violence, call a disabled person brave or inspirational, or I'll haunt you.

These are some of the words from the eulogy of Dr. Susie Balderston, who died at the end of 2023. As a disabled activist, Susie had spent much of her life fighting for the rights of disabled people. I first met her in 2010 when I was organising a conference on disability hate crime with Prof. Alan Roulstone. She pressed on me the importance of understanding the experiences of disabled women as victims of crime and how they were often ignored by policy makers and practitioners. We kept in touch over the years and often discussed allyship, how as a non-disabled academic I could contribute to activism in a respectful way. Her message was always about continuous dialogue, creating space and passing the mic. But it was also about the duty of feminists like me to be called to the struggle against the harms experienced by disabled women and not to expect them to campaign without support. Our plans to work together sadly will not come to fruition, but I will carry her powerful message with me in all of my future work.

In many discussions with Susie we talked about the field of hate studies and how it had often overlooked victim experiences which sat at the inter-section of different identities. This silo approach, which I have written about in other publications, has been mirrored in legislative responses to hate crime and has meant that groups including disabled women have frequently been ignored. It is partly why I have moved away from studying policy responses and towards the nuanced lived experiences that form the centrepiece of this book. In doing so, I became increasingly aware of the work of disability activists who have used online spaces to share the microaggressions, intrusions and hostility that they face in their daily encounters with strangers. One of these is Dr. Amy Kavanagh, whose work discussing everything from access denials to sexual assault, has challenged negative attitudes towards disability. But talking about trauma can come at a personal cost which is demonstrated by the resistance some people show online when Amy talks about what happens to her. This takes the form of invalidating her experiences of violent ableism. The criminal justice system is repeatedly shown to be lacking, not having the will or understanding to take action against perpetrators. Which again brings my own research back to a focus on the lived experience of disabled women and bearing witness to what happens to them.

The stories that follow in this book are not easy reading. They draw out the regular, unwanted ableist intrusions that disabled women often experience in their daily lives. There are discussions about physical and sexual abuse and the safety work they do to avoid them. If you are not a disabled woman then I encourage you to think about the impact of what the stories tell you and channel that shock into action. Listen to disabled women and believe them. Then think about how you might be an ally.

Brighton, UK   Hannah Mason-Bish
December 2024

Acknowledgements First I would like to thank the many participants in this study who generously shared their experiences for the project. This book would not have been possible without their carefully considered contributions and I hope the book serves to educate wider society about the daily intrusions that happen in their lives.

To my friends and colleagues who have provided advice and support throughout this project—namely Lizzie Seal, Mark Walters, Chrissie Rogers, Lis Carter and Carli Rowell. Your wise words and answers to panicked messages have not gone unnoticed. Also, to Jane Healy and Leah Burch for excellent advice on reading drafts of chapters.

My support network including Alex Bish, Beth Laybourne, Lia Oakley, Sarah Thomas, Boo Prince-Venter and my family. Huge appreciation for keeping me on track and providing tea, chocolate, cake and emergency crisis support.

To Amy Kavanagh who has influenced my work in more ways than she will ever know. Thank you for your generosity in sharing your activism with me and trusting me to work with you on this project. It's a privilege to have met and listened to you.

Last, (and definitely not least) my son Ted. When he was much younger he watched a disabled woman being 'helped' into a small aisle chair to get onto an aeroplane. He asked 'why don't they just make the doors bigger so she can use her own chair'? The innocence of his question, as yet unaware of the ableism built into the fabric of society should remind us all of what is possible. Don't ever change Ted.

Ethics Approval The study was performed in line with the principles of the Declaration of Helsinki. Approval was granted by the Ethics Committee of the University of Sussex Social Sciences and Arts Cross-Schools Research Ethics Committee (C-REC) and the LPS ethical review process. Reference ER/HM287/3. Informed consent was obtained from participants which included for research findings to be used for academic publications.

Praise for *Disability, Gender, Bodies and Boundaries*

"In light of campaigns such as 'Me Too', women have taken a stand against unwanted male advances, and yet disabled women do not get the same attention as their non-disabled peers, despite being on the receiving end of many physical intrusions. Furthermore, they are not represented in criminological work or policy documents. Hannah Mason-Bish as a feminist criminologist redresses this imbalance and uncovers the brutal reality for many disabled women. We hear stories about unwanted touch, advances and intrusions into their personal space as they go about their daily lives. This impacts their identity, their interactions with others, and how they navigate public ableist spaces. As the reader we hear about the nature of the touch, responses to advances, and even what the motivations are of the perpetrator. Significantly we also hear about their hopes and reflections. This work is wonderfully accessible, prioritises the women who participated in the research in a striking and authentic manner and critically is grounded in rigorous feminist scholarly work."
—Professor Chrissie Rogers, *School of Social Sciences, University of Kent*

"This book is a vital and eye-opening exploration of the daily intrusions faced by disabled women, from unwanted comments to physical and sexual violations. By introducing the powerful concept of "ableist intrusions," Mason-Bish exposes the harmful intersection of ableism and misogyny while aptly amplifying the voices of those most affected. A must-read for anyone committed to equity and inclusion, this book challenges societal norms, while offering a roadmap for change. It is a bold and essential contribution to feminist disability studies and beyond."

—Professor Mark Walters, *Faculty of Social Sciences, University of Sussex*

Fig. 1 Drawing by Mimi Butlin @mimibutlin Image is a drawing shows the back of a woman sat in a wheelchair with brown hair in a bob. She wears a purple jumper. A man, standing behind the chair is pushing her and there is a symbol over the handle and his hand indicating that it is wrong. Red text reads 'Do Not Touch My Aid Without My Consent. Respect My Boundaries'

CONTENTS

CHAPTER 1

Introduction

Abstract This chapter provides an overview of the book and introduces the reader to the phenomenon of ableist intrusions and how disabled women experience unwanted touching. Highlighting the research gap within both criminology and disability studies, this chapter points to the importance of adopting an intersectional approach to research. In providing the context of the way that disabled women experience abuse, violence and hostility, the chapter also emphasises the importance of incorporating their voices which are often dismissed in policy and practice. This chapter therefore explores the inspiration for the research on which this book is based and the need to understand how disabled women experience intrusive behaviours in public contexts. This book is the first piece of research to have this as a central focus and to offer new insights into this empirically underexplored issue.

Keywords Disabled women · Disability research · Ableism · Intrusion · Intersectionality

H. Mason-Bish, *Disability, Gender, Bodies and Boundaries*, Palgrave
Hate Studies, https://doi.org/10.1007/978-3-031-85890-1_1

1

BOUNDARIES AND DISABLED BODIES

We have a right to decide who touches us and when. You don't have to tolerate it or accept it when someone violates your boundaries or ignores your bodily autonomy. This doesn't have to be part of the experience of being disabled. We do not need permission to exist independently in public places, and we don't have to accept help that we don't want. (Kavanagh, 2022)

These are the words of blind activist Amy Kavanagh, describing her campaign that she set up to highlight the nature of unwanted touching that happens to her almost every day. Inspired by her own experience of becoming 'visibly disabled' when she started using a white cane, she sought to encourage others to share their stories using the Just Ask, Don't Grab hashtag. Disabled people shared a full spectrum of experiences including pulling and pushing, hitting, groping, sexual violence and harassment. The nature of touching varied depending upon impairment, location and intent but underlined the ubiquity of intrusions that disabled people face and the way that their consent is seen as unwarranted or irrelevant. While both disabled men and women reported comments, it was notable that for women, the variety of types of touching encompassed more aggressive forms of groping and sexual harassment. There was also an ever-present fear that the person grabbing them might have a sexual motive. Some activists have spoken of the more drastic actions they have taken to avoid being touched. Activist Bronwyn Berg received a lot of attention when she tweeted about an incident where a man suddenly started pushing her wheelchair and she called for help but no one intervened:

If you see a person in a wheelchair (especially a woman) being pushed by someone and she's screaming Stop! No! Help! For the love of humanity help her!

A guy grabbed my wheelchair today and just started pushing me, not a single passerby helped even though I was screaming for help. (Berg, 2019)

Her experience typifies the way that disabled women are both highly visible and frequently silenced, but their wants and needs are overlooked (Zitzelsberger, 2005). Berg has since attached spikes to the handles of her wheelchair, a very particular form of safety work that some disabled women feel forced to do.

The campaign work of disabled activists like Amy Kavanagh has been crucial in challenging the narrative of how disabled people should be able to live their lives. Many public assumptions are rooted in ableism, the idea that disabled people are deficient and in need of fixing. Such perceptions prioritise the needs of non-disabled people and lead to the exclusion of disabled people from public life (Wolbring, 2008). This can be seen in high profile activism such as the Me Too movement where disabled women were silenced and the nuances of their experiences were ignored (Palacios, 2020). This neglect has been mirrored in criminological scholarship which has typically 'excluded, pathologized or silenced' disabled voices within the field of study (Macdonald & Peacock, 2024, p. 13). Attention has certainly been paid to uncovering the nature, extent and impacts of violence against women generally. Relevant to this study, there is a broad literature base focused on the public harassment of women and their sense of safety (see e.g., Gardner, 1995; Vera-Gray, 2016). We know that women are routinely abused, shouted at, sexually propositioned and insulted when moving in public spaces. We know that women take on board 'safety work' and limit their movements because public spaces often have a terrorising effect (Vera-Gray & Kelly, 2020). Policy attention has also focused on how to help women as victims of public harassment including debates about getting misogyny recognised as a hate crime (Zempi & Smith, 2021). Yet initiatives have frequently failed to centre the experiences and voices of disabled women, or even to consider them at all (Morris, 1996; Balderston, 2013a). In short, the lack of scholarly focus on disabled women is often mirrored in policy and practice. This book addresses this omission by providing an empirically informed account of the lived experiences of disabled women and the unwanted intrusive behaviours that happen to them in public space.

An estimated 16.1 million people in the United Kingdom are disabled and 8.5 million of these are women (Kirk-Wade et al., 2024). So the need to understand the compound oppression that disabled women experience is far from a niche issue. In terms of what is known about their victimisation, in the UK, disabled women are almost twice as likely to have experienced sexual assault in the last year than women who are not disabled (ONS, 2021). They are also more likely to be violently injured during a sexual assault and less likely to receive medical care or a police response (Balderston, 2013b). Research by the TUC (2021) revealed that disabled women, particularly younger ones, are experiencing high rates of sexual harassment within the workplace (TUC, 2021). Their study found that 78% of younger disabled women had been sexually harassed at work (compared with 52% of women generally). The resultant effect is a lack of political and legal attention paid to eradicating abuse and violence towards disabled women. More often than not, the experiences of disabled women are mentioned in a footnote or a paragraph within wider violence against women policy documents. What rarely happens is an attempt to connect the different forms of violence, abuse and forced intrusion across their lives. So as well as exploring individual experiences of unwanted touching, this book will situate it within the continuum of violence that comes to punctuate and shape their lives.

There is a clear need for research into how disabled women experience intrusive behaviours in public contexts and how this impacts on their day-to-day lives. This book is the first piece of research to have this as a central focus and to offer new insights into this empirically underexplored issue. This phenomenon has been given little public policy attention and the book provides important information for policy makers who are tasked with addressing discrimination and preventing violence and harassment. I develop the concept of 'ableist intrusions' as a way of understanding and naming the problem of unwanted touching that disabled activists have been talking about in their campaign work. The aim is to use this as a reference point for the development of further scholarship on this social problem. The book argues for an intersectional approach which illuminates the nuanced lived experiences of disabled women.

The Lost Intersection

Before I acquired a physical impairment, it was sexism which dominated my interactions with the public and private world; now it is other people's reaction to me as a disabled woman which structures my experience. It is also my impairment which prevents most non-disabled women from identifying their interests with mine. (Morris, 1996, p. 3)

In the 1990s, disabled feminist Jenny Morris wrote a critique of mainstream feminism noting its failure to include disabled women in its theory, research and politics (Morris, 1992, 1996). Morris highlighted how being a disabled woman framed the way that people reacted to her, which frequently manifested as a form of exclusion from the assumed interests of non-disabled women. She expressed that this was about the way that disabled women were seen as objects rather than subjects of study. The subsequent move to establish feminist disability studies therefore sought to centre previously 'dismissed voices' and to challenge assumptions and institutions that exerted power over them. As Garland-Thomson (2001) observed, this required an understanding of the intersectional experiences of 'double discrimination', which impact most severely on the lives of disabled women leaving them 'at the corner of disability and womanhood' (Wolfe, L. in Garland-Thomson, 2001, p. i). Central to this was the call to write about and analyse personal experiences of the body and not just the social barriers to inclusion. It meant taking inspiration from both feminism and the disability movement which had often neglected to understand disabled women's experiences (Morris, 1996).

In order to address Garland-Thomson's call to identify the 'dismissed voices' of disabled women, this book utilises intersectionality to understand the way that gender and disability intertwine (Garland-Thomson, 2005, p. 1557). In Kimberlé Crenshaw's defining work (1991) on intersectionality she highlighted the 'single axis' approach to discrimination legislation which meant that policy often focused on one aspect of oppression such as race or gender and fundamentally erased the experiences of black women. Instead, she suggested that individuals, institutions and cultural practices respond to different aspects of identity and that this creates a more complex picture of discrimination. Intersectionality means considering multiple layers of group-based oppression and socio-cultural harm. Crucially, it is not about creating hierarchies of oppression but instead understanding the dynamic, lived experiences of diverse groups of women. Since its inception, intersectionality has been applied to many different aspects of identity and oppression, which Healy describes as its 'travelling appeal' (Healy, 2024, p. 25). In disability studies, innovative work by Balderston (2014) showed that disabled women face shifting inequalities relating to structural and situational discrimination. For example, disabled women are less likely to find accessible services and support after sexual violence than non-disabled women. They are also more likely to be isolated and lose financial control of their affairs meaning that leaving violent situations is more difficult (Balderston, 2014, p. 220). Intersectionality offers the chance to understand structural difficulties that make it harder for some groups of women to access support.

As an analytic tool, intersectionality has been adopted by wider feminist movements and has provided nuanced understandings of victim experiences. Saxton et al.'s. (2001) work on violence by personal assistance providers is clearly highlighted by the title of their article 'Bring me my scooter so I can leave you'. They not only showed the gendered and ableist barriers to leaving, but the specific nature of abuse which often focused on mobility aids and situational vulnerability of the disabled victim. In their work on disability and domestic violence, Thiara et al. (2011) further note that intersectionality is central to explaining the power relations that create the multiple systems of oppression which lead to abuse. It is also indicative of the need for new ways of understanding domestic violence which incorporate a more diverse array of behaviours and require different policy responses. In Healy's (2022) work on disability hate crime, she observed the way that disabled women experienced more varieties of violence than disabled men such as name calling, verbal abuse and being threatened (p. 176). In this book I will use intersectionality to bridge a gap between disability studies and feminist scholarship in this area to argue that new ways of understanding the phenomenon of unwanted touching are essential to combatting it. The book is cautious to avoid a form of 'lazy intersectionality' which might prioritise one aspect of identity over another, or claims that there is one experience that all disabled women share (Watermeyer & Swartz, 2022). Its utility is in demonstrating that intersectional experiences can be dynamic and situational.

Focus of the Book

This book empirically evidences the problem of unwanted touching that disabled women experience on a regular basis. I take a phenomenological approach to understand their lived and embodied experiences and develop the concept of ableist intrusions. While Calder-Dawe et al. (2019) use the term as a loose way of describing the nature of everyday ableism, I seek to ground it more concretely in the work of Fiona Vera-Gray, to show how it operates at the intersection of gender and disability. Ableist intrusions happen because strangers feel more confident to assess, critique and interrupt the bodies of disabled women in particular ways. Further-more, their impacts include additional safety work, which encompass both practical changes to daily life and a deeper management of the self. In seeking to explain this, I use the findings of an exploratory study that I conducted to gather stories from disabled women. In total, 80 narratives were received, and the subsequent chapters are based on the words and accounts of the participants themselves. The decision to focus on how intrusions are embodied was influenced by the work of disability rights campaigner Lois Keith. Writing about her own encounters with strangers, Keith contributed a chapter to a book by Jenny Morris where she gath-ered together a number of her personal stories in order to explain the nature of what happened to her on a regular basis (Keith, 1996). The result is a powerful piece of writing which demonstrates the way that interruptions are felt emotionally, physically and psychologically. Keith noted:

> If you bring any group of disabled people together, before too long we'll be swapping stories about the annoying, appalling, patronising, insensitive, unhelpful and sometimes just plain funny encounters that we have on an almost daily basis. (Keith, 1996, p. 70)

The chapters that follow draw together such narratives in the hope of improving understanding about the continuum of unwanted ableist intrusions and how these shape the lives of disabled women.

CHAPTER STRUCTURE

The book begins by providing an overview of academic literature looking at gender and disability in the context of crime, abuse and violence. Using feminist disability studies as a starting point, the chapter examines the importance of the social model of disability for providing the broader context of ableism. The chapter shows that disabled women are more likely to experience violence and abuse yet less likely to have this recog-nised publicly and politically. It discusses the ways in which public space is ableist space which works to exclude disabled people and how women's bodies are subject to scrutiny. The chapter also assesses issues of acces-sibility and inclusion which present particular barriers. These are framed within the wider context of ableism and stereotypes about who should be in public space.

Chapter 3 outlines the methodological approach of the project which was grounded in feminist disability studies. The method involved developing a WordPress site where women could share their stories of unwanted and non-consensual touching. The chapter discusses the practicalities of the approach and provides research reflections about using a narrative method to gather and share the stories of participants. This chapter also examines the issue of positionality and how the insider/outsider status of the author framed the research process. As a non-disabled researcher the project was developed and carried out working closely with a visually impaired activist who advised on appropriate methodologies, language and sampling. The chapter also reflects on the theme of intersectionality by demonstrating how this was central to an inclusive research process.

Chapter 4 outlines the concept of ablest intrusions by detailing the experiences of disabled women and the daily behaviours that happen to them. The chapter demonstrates how these are regular, constant and daily interruptions in public space. Ranging from intrusive comments to violence and sexual assault, the chapter provides a detailed and rich description of the experience of ableist intrusions. This also includes a discussion of how these experiences are embodied and how disabled women feel objectified and infantilised by what happens. As the chapter proceeds it situates these within the context of disability stereotypes to show that intrusions are part of a broader societal attitude towards disability which reinforces ableist ideas.

In Chapter 5 I offer a deeper examination of the ableist nature of public space. This will focus on who is doing the intruding and what their potential motivations say about how disabled women are viewed. The research revealed how perpetrators were from a broad spectrum of society and when challenged would often excuse their behaviour as being helpful. Such benevolent ableism drew on stereotypes of disabled people as weak and in need of assistance. For participants who experienced sexual abuse from men, the motivation was similarly dismissed based on the notion that disabled women were not sexual beings who must have misunderstood what was happening. These findings are examined in relation to the intersection of gender and disability and how some bodies are seen as desirable, damaged and /or weak. The chapter starts to tease out the emotional labour required of disabled women by looking at their reactions to ableist intrusions.

Chapter 6 details the impacts of ableist intrusions and shows how disabled women limit their daily movements in order to avoid intrusive behaviours. This means changing routes home even when these are less accessible or forgoing their mobility aid so as not to appear visibly disabled. This has significant impacts on their physical and emotional wellbeing and is often in addition to injuries sustained during the unwanted intrusions where disabled women might be placed in danger or have serious harm caused to them. Importantly, this chapter also explores the deeper ontological impacts on disabled women and their sense of self.

The final chapter draws together and clarifies what is meant by the term ableist intrusion and how it is a personal, embodied experience which forces disabled women to live smaller lives. They are marked out as hyper visible in public space and in need of help, yet their consent is not sought and autonomy is denied. The gendered fear of public space is wrapped around its ableist atmosphere. The chapter reminds the reader of the safety work and emotional labour required of disabled women and also their hopes for future change.

References

Balderston, S. (2013a). After disablist hate crime: Which interventions really work to resist victimhood and build resilience with survivors? In A. Roulstone & H. Mason-Bish (Eds.), *Disability, hate crime and violence* (pp. 177–192). Routledge.

Balderston, S. (2013b). Victimised again? Intersectionality and injustice in disabled women's lives after hate crime and rape. In M. Texler Segal, & V. Demos (Eds.), *Gendered perspectives on conflict and violence: Part A*. Advances in Gender Research, Volume 18A (pp. 17–51). Emerald Group Publishing Ltd.

Balderston, S. (2014). *Surviving disablist hate rape: Barriers, intersectionalities and collective interventions with disabled women in the North of England* (Doctoral Thesis, Lancaster University). Lancaster University.

Berg, B. [@bergbronwyn]. (2019, January 13). *If you see a person in a wheelchair (especially a woman) being pushed by someone and she's screaming Stop! No! [Post]*. Twitter. https://twitter.com/bergbronwyn/status/108424 0379535392769

Calder-Dawe, O., Witten, K., & Carroll, P. (2019). Being the body in question: young people's accounts of everyday ableism, visibility and disability. *Disability & Society, 35*(1), 132–155. https://doi.org/10.1080/09687599. 2019.1621742

Crenshaw, K. (1991, July). Mapping the margins: Intersectionality, identity politics, and violence against women of color. *Stanford Law Review, 43*(6), 1241–1299

Gardner, C. B. (1995). *Passing by: Gender and public harassment*. University of California Press.

Garland-Thomson, R. (2001). *Re-shaping, re-thinking, re-defining: Feminist disability studies, The Barbara Waxman Fiduccia Papers on Women and Girls with Disabilities*. Center for Women Policy Studies. https://bpb-us-e2.wpm ucdn.com/sites.middlebury.edu/dist/1/4371/files/2020/03/Garland-Tho mson_Redefining_Feminist_Disabilities_Studies_2001.pdf

Garland-Thomson, R. (2005). Feminist disability studies: A review of essays. *Signs, 30*(2), 1557–1587.

Healy, J. (2022). Examining disability hate crime. In J. Healy, & B. Colliver (Eds.), *Contemporary intersectional criminology in the UK examining the boundaries of intersectionality and crime*. Policy Press.

Healy, J. (2024). Revealing the benefits, barriers, and prevalence of intersectionality in disability hate crime research. In L. Burch, & D. Wilkin (Eds.), *Disability hate crime: Perspectives for change*. Routledge.

Kavanagh, A. (2022). *Hands off: Navigating unwanted touch, consent and disability, University of Oxford annual disability lecture* [Transcript]. https:// podcasts.ox.ac.uk/2022-disability-lecture-hands-navigating-unwanted-touch-consent-and-disability. Accessed 26 September 2024.

Keith, L. (1996). Encounters with strangers: The public's responses to disabled women and how this affects our sense of self. In J. Morris (Ed.), *Encounters with strangers: Feminism and disability* (pp. 69–89). The Women's Press.

Kirk-Wade, E., Stiebahl, S., & Wong, H. (2024). *UK disability statistics: Prevalence and life experiences, research briefing*, 2 October 2024, House of Common Library.

MacDonald, S. J., & Peacock, D. (2024). Dis/ableist criminology: Applying disability theory within a criminological context. In K. J. Stockdale, & M. Addison (Eds.), *Marginalised voices in criminology* (pp. 13–31). Routledge.

Morris, J. (1992). Personal and political: A feminist perspective on researching physical disability. *Disability, Handicap & Society, 7*, 157–166.

Morris, J. (1996). *Encounters with strangers: Feminism and disability*. The Women's Press.

Office for National Statistics. (2021). *Sexual offences victim characteristics, England and Wales: Year ending March 2021*. Retrieved October 11, 2024 from https://www.ons.gov.uk/peoplepopulationandcommunity/crimeandj ustice/articles/sexualoffencesvictimcharacteristicsenglandandwales/march2 020#disability

Palacios, M. (2020, February 19). *Why disabled women haven't joined the Me too movement*. Retrieved October 10, 2024, from https://www.audacitymaga zine.com/why-disabled-women-havent-joined-the-me-too-movement/

Saxton, M., Curry, M., Powers, L. E., Maley, S., Eckels, K., & Gross, J. (2001). 'Bring My Scooter So I Can Leave You': A study of disabled women handling abuse by personal assistance providers. *Violence Against Women, 7*(4), 393–417. https://doi.org/10.1177/1077801012218252

Thiara, R., Hague, G., & Mullender, A. (2011). Losing out on both counts: Disabled women and domestic violence. *Disability & Society, 26*(6), 757–771. https://doi.org/10.1080/09687599.2011.602867

TUC. (2021). *Sexual harassment of disabled women in the workplace*. Retrieved October 10, 2024 from https://www.tuc.org.uk/sites/default/files/2021-07/DisabledWomenSexual%20harassmentReport.pdf

Watermeyer, B., & Swartz, L. (2022). Disability and the problem of lazy inter-sectionality. *Disability & Society, 38*(2), 362–366. https://doi.org/10.1080/09687599.2022.2130177

Vera-Gray, F. (2016). Men's stranger intrusions: Rethinking street harassment. *Women's Studies International Forum., 58*, 9–17.

Vera-Gray, F., & Kelly, L. (2020). Contested gendered space: Public sexual harassment and women's safety work. *International Journal of Comparative and Applied Criminal Justice, 44*(4), 265–275. https://doi.org/10.1080/01924036.2020.1732435

Wolbring, G. (2008). The politics of ableism. *Development, 51*, 252–258. https://doi.org/10.1057/dev.2008.17

Zempi, I., & Smith, J. (Eds.). (2021). *Misogyny as hate crime* (1st ed.). Routledge. https://doi.org/10.4324/9781003023722

Zitzelsberger, H. (2005). (In)visibility: Accounts of embodiment of women with physical disabilities and differences. *Disability & Society, 20*(4), 389–403. https://doi.org/10.1080/09687590500086492

CHAPTER 2

The Lost Intersection: Examining Gender and Disability

Abstract The chapter will establish the conceptual framework upon which the following empirical exploration is based. It identifies the current evidence gap on disability and gender as well as outlining existing work on disablism and ableism which this study builds on. The chapter will also demonstrate the ways in which public space is structured as ableist space, which works to exclude disabled people. Issues of accessibility and inclusion are shown to present particular barriers that are framed within the wider context of ableism and stereotypes about who should access public space. Noting Jenny (Morris, 1993) critique that mainstream feminist approaches to violence often failed to include disabled women in their theory and politics, the chapter will situate the project as part of the call to include dismissed voices. Centrally, it will be shown that disabled women are more likely to experience violence and abuse, yet less likely to have this recognised publicly and politically.

Keywords Ableism · Intersectionality · Embodiment · Disability studies · Disabled women

© The Author(s), under exclusive license to Springer Nature Switzerland AG 2025
H. Mason-Bish, *Disability, Gender, Bodies and Boundaries,* Palgrave Hate Studies, https://doi.org/10.1007/978-3-031-85890-1_2

13

ABLEISM AND DISABILITY STUDIES

The prejudice and hostility that disabled people face is something that can be charted across the life course. From early experiences of exclusion in education to the forced intimacy of medical procedures and public instances of hostility, discriminatory practices come to form the basis of the lived experience of being disabled (Oliver, 1990; Oliver & Barnes, 2012). Greater awareness of these lived experiences emerged within the field of disability studies during the 1990s. A critique of the study of disability until the 1970s was that it had been overly focused on personal tragedy and the medical model of impairment. This approach meant that the disability was seen as the reason for someone's exclusion from society and attempts to include them were often individualised. Policy and discourse was framed around personal struggles and seen as the most important aspect of someone's identity, creating low expectations and a general acceptance that life would be difficult. From the 1970s onwards, such perceptions were challenged by disability studies which represented a merging of social science, anthropology, social work and various other disciplines. Rooted in activism, disability studies challenged the idea of the normal/abnormal body. In Berger's description:

> It is a way for people with disabilities to stare back at those who have stared at them (Fries, 1997), to turn society's gaze back on itself and point out the things that nondisabled people don't seem to notice because, as Davis observes, they "see themselves as living in a mirage of being normal (2005, p. 3)". (Berger, 2013, p. 4)

Central to this has been the development of the social model of disability. Coined by Mike Oliver, this model describes the process of disablement which goes beyond individual bodily impairment (Oliver, 1983; UPIAS, 1976). Since its inception, the increased awareness about how society, institutions and structures put up barriers to disabled people's participation has been used to improve employment rights, healthcare, education and civic involvement. Activists used the word 'disablism' to embody the social and structural prejudices experienced by disabled people, utilising this understanding of disability discrimination to lobby local and national governments to reorientate how disability and disabled people are defined and treated within legislative and policy-based frameworks.

As with racism, sexism and homophobia, disablism highlights behaviours and beliefs which see one group of people as superior to another because of an identity characteristic. Abuse, negative opinions and exclusionary behaviours form the basis on which it is enacted. As a concept, disablism has been useful for exposing discrimination experienced by disabled people in contexts including education, healthcare, criminal justice and transport. Scholars such as Wolbring (2008) suggest that ableism as a concept has a slightly different focus. It reflects 'a preference for species- typical normative abilities leading to the discrimination against them as "less able" and/or as "impaired" disabled people (2008, p. 253)'. Particular abilities are valued and promoted above others and it is one of the most 'societally entrenched and accepted isms' (Wolbring, 2008, p. 253). More recently, activists such as Talila Lewis have expanded this definition to detail the umbrella of isms that Wolbring was talking about:

> A system that places value on people's bodies and minds based on societally constructed ideas of normality, intelligence, excellence, desirability, and productivity. These constructed ideas are deeply rooted in anti-Blackness, eugenics, misogyny, colonialism, imperialism and capitalism. (Lewis, 2021)

This conceptualisation allows an understanding of how non-disabled people are favoured, how their bodies are seen as normative and highlights the way that the disabled body is 'out of place'. Lewis' definition also allows for a greater understanding about how the intersections of other aspects of identity are more likely to be judged as abnormal and lacking desirability. There is a narrow range of bodies that are deemed acceptable and these tend to focus on normative appearances of maleness, whiteness and heterosexuality (Zitzelsberger, 2005). Women's bodies are 'highly marked' and 'evaluated by gendered and sexual norms' (Zitzelsberger, 2005, p. 400). How gender and disability interplay in the way that bodies are seen as having the right to occupy public space is an important focus for this book and one that remains relatively under researched.

The emergence of different models of understanding disability has contributed to a large body of work which highlights how disabled people are subject to violence and harm. Katharine Quarmby's groundbreaking book *Scapegoat* (2011) charted the history of public discomfort with disability from the Ancient Greeks to the twenty-first century, drawing out particular themes which have come to characterise how disabled people are treated. These include discussions over eradicating disabled people altogether through sterilisation, aborting disabled foetuses, assisted dying and euthanasia debates. Other themes include how worthwhile disabled lives can be, the cost implications to society and whether adaptations should be required in order to facilitate accessible and inclusive spaces. Quarmby also discusses the exclusionary practices, sometimes mandated in law, which moved disabled people from public freakshows to grim, sequestered asylums where they were no longer in the view of the public. High profile instances of abuse in care settings exposed institutional failures and often non-existent safeguards which enabled a culture of disablist violence to proliferate.

Journalist John Pring investigated the scandal at Longcare home for disabled people, where a leaked council report had revealed that residents who were learning disabled had been routinely beaten, neglected and raped (Pring, 2003). Continued scandals in care home settings have shown repetitive patterns of devaluing behaviour and the dehumanisation of disabled residents. In these environments, disabled people can routinely experience infringements on their personal liberty, control of their intimate care and decisions over who they are able to socialise with. More broadly, the limitations put on their individual freedoms are framed as being essential safeguarding practices. These are deemed necessary to protect individuals' 'vulnerability', meaning that the criminal justice system is not seen as a suitable option for disabled people to access. For disabled women in particular, non-consensual touching in institutional care settings are also explained away as being 'either for their own good or the good of society' (Rohrer, 2005, p. 50). Disabled women and girls are socialised that such behaviour is a normal part of life.

As activists uncovered the violence happening behind closed doors it has been a more recent development that hostility on the streets has come to wider attention. Disabled people regularly experience hostility which includes verbal abuse, physical violence and threatening behaviour (Healy, 2019; Wilkin, 2020). They are attacked by strangers, acquaintances and those who have befriended them with intent to abuse (Thomas, 2011). Over 190 legal jurisdictions around the world have passed legislation to recognise abuse based on different forms of prejudice and added sentencing provisions for particular groups (Walters, 2022). In England and Wales, disability has been included in the list of groups afforded that protection since 2003 and in the period to 2023–2024 there were 11,719 disability hate crimes recorded by the police in England and Wales

(Home Office, 2024). Yet only 311 cases were prosecuted. In what can be described as a justice gap for disabled people, crimes targeting them are routinely dismissed as being about vulnerability rather than hate (Mason-Bish, 2013). This protectionist approach relates to the assumption that disabled people lack power and agency and are vulnerable in all settings and at all times. This has been widely critiqued by academics in the field of hate studies who have noted that disability has not been fully embraced by the hate crime policy domain (Mason-Bish, 2013).

Stereotypes and Disabled Bodies

The violence and abuse facing disabled people is rooted in emotions, which Bill Hughes specifies as fear, pity and disgust (Hughes, 2012). Describing these as the 'building blocks of the emotional infrastructure of ableism' these frame the social distance between disabled and non-disabled people (p. 68). Writing in 1998, Morgan Brown provided detail about how this can lead to 'destructive assumptions' which foster the abuse of disabled people including:

1. Difference as bad, inferior and devalued
2. Disability means without ability, dignity, pride or dreams
3. Incompetent to provide for and direct their own lives
4. Vulnerability is a fault, a symptom that something is wrong with a person
5. It is acceptable to exclude them from decisions in or affecting their own lives
6. Non-disabled people always know what is best for disabled people
7. Individual personal value is measured by net material worth, not personal existence (Brown, 1998 as in Calderbank, 2000, p. 525).

These assumptions not only provide the justification for abuse and infringements on the personal space of disabled people, but they also create the climate in which perpetrators of abuse are not prosecuted or punished. Disabled people can become infantilised due to having their autonomy taken over decisions involving their care, health and personal wellbeing. This is particularly acute for disabled women who are more likely to be viewed as lacking capacity. As Garland-Thomson says, 'female, disabled, and dark bodies are supposed to be dependent, incomplete, vulnerable and incompetent bodies' (2002, p. 7). This idea of inherent ineptitude also provides the gateway for infringements on personal liberty. For Hughes (2012), disabled people are seen as deserving of sympathy when cast as unfortunates and this creates an environment of pity and charity (Hughes, 2012, p. 70). This is a necessarily hierarchical emotion, measured by comparing a disabled body against a non-disabled one. With the philanthropy of charity also comes applause for giving help above and beyond what is expected. In terms of being a carer, public discourse portrays this role as bearing a burden of looking after a disabled person in what is seen as a thankless, tiring and exhausting role. This furthers a rhetoric of power imbalance where a disabled person should be grateful for the help received because of their vulnerability. For disabled women, these forms of disbelief are framed around their gender and disability 'because some professionals do not recognise disabled women's capacity for sexual and intimate relationships or because carers are regarded as being beyond reproach' (Nixon, 2009, p. 82). As this book progresses, this theme of benevolent ableism as it relates to disability and gender will become increasingly significant.

A further stereotype of disabled bodies is that they are defective and in need of cure and treatment. Theorists of embodiment note a focus on the leaky, malfunctioning body as a site of threat and disgust. For disabled women, this is compounded by the fact that women's bodies generally are subject to regulation and control, with basic bodily functions seen as disgusting (Shildrick, 1997). Garland-Thomson's (2005) work on the representation of disability in culture highlights how they are represented as a form of corporeal deviance with a focus on what they lack. This leads to low expectations for disabled people and public surprise when they might be doing routine activities like shopping, driving or working (Nario-Redmond et al., 2019). Again, the intersection of gender and disability is important because societal expectations are lower for disabled women than disabled men:

> cultural assumptions about disability that entails weakness, dependency, and helplessness clash with cultural assumptions of masculinity, but overlap cultural assumptions of femininity so that a disabled man is perceived as a 'wounded male', while a disabled woman is redundantly fulfilling cultural expectations of her. This further shows how disability and illness are gendered feminine. (Ahlvik-Harju, 2016, p. 227)

Activist and writer Nancy Mairs noted that people with 'whole bodies' would mistake disabled people for 'heroes' when doing basic daily tasks (Mairs, 1996). These representations serve to make the non-disabled public feel good about their own able bodies but also lead them to be critical of people who cannot overcome their adversity. These stereotypes result in persistent discourses that some disabled people are lazy and could make greater efforts to work and contribute to society. In Frances Ryan's text *Crippled* (2019), she details the horrifying effects of austerity and financial cuts to services which have resulted in suffering, further disablement and death. Such ongoing cuts are only possible to justify by sending the message that disabled people need to try harder and earn their place in society. This of course contributes to a societal atmosphere where disability is not welcome and disabled bodies are 'out of place'. Its message is transmitted through cultural representations, government policy and the physical design of towns and cities.

DISABILITY AND PUBLIC SPACE

Freedom of movement and belonging in public space is not something that disabled people have access to. It is a site of emotional labour, where access is granted inconsistently. The social model of disability has done much to demonstrate the ways that accessibility in towns and cities is limited, sending the message that disabled people are not welcome to move freely in public space. The work of human geographers within disability studies has provided a rich literature here, calling to question the spatial designs within mainstream society that work both practically and culturally to keep disabled people out. Rob Kitchin's defining work on disability and public space described these practices:

> Implicit or thoughtless designs include the use of steps with no ramp; cash machines being placed too high; places linked by inaccessible public transport. Such practices are enshrined in, and perpetuated by, the planning system. (Kitchin, 1998, p. 347)

Imrie (1996) speaks of this as a design apartheid which 'lock' disabled people out. Although this work was written in the 1990s, public space continues to prioritise the needs of the able-bodied community. A recent example of this can be seen in the state-mandated control of public areas during the Covid-19 pandemic. In Britain, the 2020–2021 rule that people must maintain a social distance of 2 metres when out in public was practically challenging for many disabled people navigating narrow pavements. The Royal National Institute for the Blind (RNIB) reported that blind and visually impaired people found it impossible to navigate new one-way layouts, signage and additional hazards which were made worse by members of the public confronting them about it (RNIB, 2020). The slow reopening of public areas, which included encouraging outdoor restaurant dining, meant that pavements were clogged with chairs and tables, again restricting the movement of people with physical impairment. The subtext of the design of civic space serves 'to convince disabled people that they are "out of place" and to keep them "in their place"' (Kitchin, 1998, p. 354). Access denials and difficulties also signify to non-disabled people that certain bodies do not have the legitimacy to exist in particular spaces.

The RNIB report on effects of Covid-19 regulations on blind and partially sighted people pointed to the way that government rules fostered an environment where people were encouraged to challenge and police disabled people who might be breaking the rules. This was accompanied by advice that vulnerable people should shield at home in order to protect themselves. The result was a climate in which disabled bodies should be hidden from view in order to prioritise the needs of non-disabled people. It is in this context that ableism helps to explain the daily experiences of disabled people and a small number of scholars have highlighted particular themes. Calder-Dawe et al.'s research on young people with sensory impairments described how 'everyday ableism reflects broader sociocultural relations of power, while also being a profoundly personal, relational and embodied experience' (2019, p. 135). In these seemingly mundane encounters, the disabled body becomes highly visible, with mobility aids representing emblems of weakness. White canes and assistance dogs allow strangers to perform a 'diagnostic' assessment of the disabled person which can then lead to personal and intrusive questions about their impairment. They become a focal point of interaction with strangers (Edwards & Maxwell, 2021, p. 168). In a more hostile escalation, this can also result in a challenge and judgement, focused on disabled parking spaces or offering unwanted advice on how to operate their own mobility aid (Calder-Dawe et al., 2019). Public transport can be a particularly contested space, where disabled people find themselves subject to abuse and discrimination by both transport staff and strangers (Wayland et al., 2020).

Researchers have illustrated how some aspects of ableism in public space are more closely related to specific elements of impairment. In Lenney and Sercombe's (2002) study on wheelchair users in pubs they detail how the social context of a drinking establishment is seen as a space where disabled people do not go. Hughes (1999) describes the non-disabled gaze as a 'specific way of seeing which actually constructs the world it claims to have discovered' (p. 155). Ellis' (2017) research on people with dwarfism highlighted the way that strangers would take unauthorised photographs of them. Their 'unusual' presence and visibility combines with long-standing histories of mocking and ridicule which leads to strangers feeling entitled to photograph them. These encounters have a significant emotional labour for disabled people who may change routes or locations to avoid the intrusive staring or comments by people. They might wear cameras in order to record or prepare for incidents of hostility (Edwards & Maxwell, 2021, p. 170). A management of the self such as this includes trying to be invisible and out of sight, out of mind (McClimens et al., 2014). Zitzelsberger's (2005) work details how disabled women experience the built environment in particular ways, with their bodies being hypervisible, yet their desires and agency were unseen. When occupying spaces where their equipment or access needs were accommodated, their bodies were less visible and less of a focal point for interaction. Yet this can work in contradictory ways. In Wayland et al.'s (2020) research on young disabled people using public transport, they found that when women had less visible disabilities they were more likely to be challenged about their right to use a concession ticket or receive abuse for not stopping a bus in time.

The ableist world, enacted in encounters with strangers, has a real impact on the inner existence of disabled people. Instances of forced help exist because disabled people are not seen as 'active-doers' and instead are 'objects of benefaction' (Loja et al., 2012, p. 193). These perceptions have impacts which have been described as psycho-emotional disablism. Coined by Carol Thomas (1999) it describes the negative impacts on self esteem and confidence, but also ontological invalidation (Reeve, 2012). Behaviours which become so commonplace that they are internalised lead to disabled people having negative perceptions of themselves. It is here that phenomenological approaches have brought greater understanding to bodily awareness and its relevance to disability studies. Paterson and Hughes suggest that negative and hostile experiences produce an 'unwanted consciousness of one's impaired body'

(1999, p. 603) where the body is brought to the fore in particular encounters with strangers. The disabled person is not just confronted by prejudice, they are also confronted by themselves and their 'impaired body dys-appears' (p. 603). The notion of the dys-appearing body is drawn from the work of Leder (1990) who theorised that in daily life our bodies disappear so that we are not subjectively aware of them and they recede into the background. If something goes wrong, such as pain or injury then they dys-appear and come to the forefront of our attention. This can be used to explain the psycho-emotional disablism when life is interrupted by strangers critiquing, targeting and abusing the disabled body. But it also presents a deeper ontological challenge. Researchers have pushed back against the idea of disabled people as pathological victims and to demonstrate how the dys-appearing body can become a site of resistance and agency. In Loja et al.'s (2012) study of embodiment and disability, participants spoke of re-engaging a positive identity in relation to their bodies, their mobility aids and their relationships with other people. Identity is an embodied construction (2012, p. 202). In relation to disabled women, an underexplored area is the ways in which gender and disability form the embodied experience of being in public and how their bodies are invalidated by strangers in intersectional ways.

Gendered Spaces and Disabled Women

If public space is ableist space, then it is also gendered. While feminist scholars and activists worked to highlight the interpersonal violence and abuse happening in homes and relationships, this meant that sometimes the public sphere was overlooked. Vera-Gray and Kelly (2020) note that public space was not always seen as a 'conducive context' in which violence and harassment could happen. They argue that public space is gendered space and that women are often tasked with taking on a repertoire of safety measures to mitigate against that risk. This is centred around perceptions of fear of crime and assessing the likelihood of violence when moving about in public. Interestingly, in some ways, the activist work by campaigners mirrors that of the disability movement as it has been about protest, access and defining who has the right to move freely in public space. Other scholars have examined this, often using the term 'street harassment' to encompass a range of behaviours. Gardner (1995) provides a comprehensive definition:

A group of abuses, harryings, and annoyances characteristic of public places and uniquely facilitated by communication in public. Public harassment includes pinching, slapping, hitting, shouted remarks, vulgarity, insults, sly innuendo, ogling, and stalking. Public harassment is on a continuum of possible events, beginning when customary civility among strangers is abrogated and ending with the transition to violent crime: assault, rape, or murder. (p. 4)

Many researchers have unpicked the motivation of street harassers and point towards the power of misogyny and the terrorising impact that unwanted behaviours can have on women. A common theme is that the intent of the harasser is mostly hidden behind a feigned compliment (Bowman, 1993; Davis, 1993). Constructed in norms of sexual behaviour, the female body is subject to commentary and the male gaze, meaning that women are quite literally 'up for grabs'. The female victim is overreacting or misunderstanding the intent which is commonly portrayed as 'men being men'.

Feminist literature on street harassment has often failed to incorporate the experiences of disabled women. Disabled feminist activists have commented on how these frameworks are unhelpful in understanding their experiential lives in public places. In 'Nobody Catcalls the Woman in the Wheelchair', Kayla Whaley writes about how she feels excluded from the discourse that suggests street harassment is ubiquitous:

I'm a wheelchair user: a visibly, physically disabled woman. And my wheelchair acts as a strange sort of forcefield. People register "disabled" before they register "woman" and the former always overrides the latter, because in our ableist society, a disabled body is necessarily a desexualized one. We are grotesque or tragic, freaks or angels, to be either feared or pitied depending on how the abled gaze lands that day. No matter what, though, we are not desirable. (Whaley, 2016)

Whaley's writing calls into question the perception of the female body as an object of sexual attraction worthy of the male gaze. The sexual lives of disabled women have been described as a 'missing discourse' in academic literature, with ableist assumptions about who is attractive (Santos & Santos, 2018). Nixon describes this as a dangerous perception because 'the perceived silence, invisibility and asexuality of disabled women, while not the cause of violence against them, can make it much more difficult to disclose or escape the violence' (Nixon, 2009, p. 82).

While feminist scholars have rightly pointed out that street harassment and stranger intrusions are about power and patriarchal control, public conceptions remain that women can be safe by limiting their movements and clothing. Women can avoid it by dressing differently, not going out after dark or being accompanied by a friend. For disabled women, these discourses—rightly or wrongly—do not include a broader consideration of motives that encompass their experiences. Public safety work involving self defence classes, taking different routes or going out in groups takes on a different emphasis when talking about women who might be visually impaired or wheelchair users. It is in this conception that we immediately see what Garland-Thomson (2002) was talking about in the way that understanding the experiences of disabled women adds nuances, depth and breadth to feminist studies. Ahlvik-Harju writes about the need for 'counter narratives that can serve to challenge the cultural narratives blurring our imaginations of disabled (and female) personhood' (2016, p. 227). Investigating the lived experience of street harassment and unwanted touching for disabled women could provide the opportunity to counter such dominant narratives and assumptions about them.

What begins to emerge is the way that more nuanced frameworks and conceptualisations are required to understand the experiences of disabled women in public spaces. It is here that the work of Fiona Vera-Gray provides an excellent entry point. In developing the concept of men's stranger intrusions, she notes the need to move towards understanding both ordinary and extraordinary interruptions into the daily lives of women. These might not feel like harassment, but they are unwanted (Vera-Gray, 2016):

> There is no need to evidence a desire to harm or disrupt the target, the focus is on the deliberateness of the practice, whilst 'uninvited' shifts from 'unwanted' as a qualifier that affirms the power of the target to choose who is able to enter their physical and emotional space. It foregrounds the actions of the perpetrator, rather than their intentions or the target's response, allowing for a broader range of practices to be addressed. (Vera-Gray, 2016, p. 11)

Drawing on the work of Liz Kelly (1988), Vera-Gray suggests that men's intrusive practices exist on a continuum across the life course. Women learn early on that such experiences are 'normal' and are taught to regulate themselves, their bodies and their movements. It marks out significant additional safety practices required of women and the way that bodies are observed and critiqued. In seeking to examine how disabled women experienced unwanted touching in public, this study will utilise the concept of intrusion in order to develop a continuum of ableist behaviours which punctuate their lives.

ABLEISM AND FEMINIST DISABILITY STUDIES: A CONCEPTUAL BASE

The work of feminist disability studies scholars has begun to unpack the treatment of disabled women at the hands of the state and wider society. Portrayed as broken, leaky and damaged, the disabled woman's body is subject to scrutiny and in need of being controlled (Shildrick, 1997). The impaired female body is therefore not sexually attractive (Santos & Santos, 2018). These portrayals combine in such a way that disabled women are denied agency and control over their bodies in many aspects of their lives. And yet sexism and disablism intersect in complex ways, as Garland-Thomson describes:

> Women are the proper object of the male gaze, while disabled people are the proper object of the stare. Beauty contests, girlie shows, freak shows, telethons, and medical theater all testify to an appropriating to-be-looked-atness that supposedly inheres in the female and or the disabled body. Leering at women and gawking at disabled people are historical practices that constitute female and disabled personhood in the social world. (Garland-Thomson, 2001, p. 9)

The extent to which disabled women experience unwanted gaze, touch and intrusion in public spaces remains an underexplored area. That feminist studies and violence against women campaigns have often overlooked this is something of a surprise given their focus on embodiment and the physical self. While there is now a significant literature examining the harassment and unwanted touching of non-disabled women, a gap remains in exploring how disabled women might experience such intrusions. How these combine elements of both misogyny and ableism is the central focus for this book.

This chapter also looked at the way that public space is ableist towards disabled men and women. Access issues and access denials continue to send messages of exclusion. To grant access is to be benevolent and to help a disabled person is to be a hero. These perceptions have been framed through decades of stereotypes and the medical model of disability which points towards pity and charity. Again, there appears to be a contradiction in that while there is a perception that disabled people need help, research shows that help in the form of access, advice and tolerance is not forthcoming. Indeed disability studies work has shown that frequently to be disabled in public is to be subject to hostility, microaggression and abuse. As this book will demonstrate, this is a fundamental aspect of ableism and sexism whereby certain bodies are afforded help and a place in public space, but this is granted on specific terms. The next chapter sets out the methodological approach for the study on which this book is based and how I incorporated 'dismissed voices' in the search to understand how disabled women experience unwanted touching in public places.

References

Ahlvik-Harju, C. (2016). Disturbing bodies—Reimagining comforting narratives of embodiment through feminist disability studies. *Scandinavian Journal of Disability Research, 18*(3), 222–233. https://doi.org/10.1080/15017419. 2015.1063545

Berger, R. J. (2013). *Introducing disability studies.* Lynne Reiner Publishers.

Bowman, C. (1993). Street harassment and the Informal ghettoization of women. *Harvard Law Review, 106*(3), 517–580. https://doi.org/10.2307/1341656

Calder-Dawe, O., Witten, K., & Carroll, P. (2019). Being the body in question: Young people's accounts of everyday ableism, visibility and disability. *Disability & Society, 35*(1), 132–155. https://doi.org/10.1080/09687599. 2019.1621742

Calderbank, R. (2000). Abuse and disabled people: Vulnerability or social indifference? *Disability & Society, 15*(3), 521–534. https://doi.org/10.1080/713661966

Davis, D. E. (1993). The harm that has no name: Street harassment, embodiment, and African American women. *UCLA Women's Law Journal, 4*(2), 133–178.

Edwards, C., & Maxwell, N. (2021). Disability, hostility and everyday geographies of un/safety. *Social & Cultural Geography, 24*(1), 157–174. https://doi.org/10.1080/14649365.2021.1950823

Ellis, L. (2017). Through a filtered lens: Unauthorized picture-taking of people with dwarfism in public spaces. *Disability & Society, 33*(2), 218–237. https://doi.org/10.1080/09687599.2017.1392930

Gardner, C. B. (1995). *Passing by: Gender and public harassment.* University of California Press.

Fries, K. (Ed.). (1997). *Staring back: The disability experience from the inside out.* Plume.

Garland-Thomson, R. (2001). Re-shaping, re-thinking, re-defining: Feminist disability studies. In *The Barbara Waxman Fiduccia papers on women and girls with disabilities.* Center for Women Policy Studies. https://bpb-us-e2.wpmucdn.com/sites.middlebury.edu/dist/1/4371/files/2020/03/Garland-Thomson_Redefining_Feminist_Disabilities_Studies_2001.pdf

Garland-Thomson, R. (2002). Integrating disability, transforming feminist theory. *NWSA Journal, 14*(3), 1–32.

Garland-Thomson, R. (2005). Feminist disability studies: A review of essays. *Signs, 30*(2), 1557–1587.

Healy, J. (2019). 'It spreads like a creeping disease': Experiences of victims of disability hate crimes in austerity Britain. *Disability & Society, 35*(2), 176–200. https://doi.org/10.1080/09687599.2019.1624151

Home Office. (2024). *Hate crime England and Wales, year ending March 2024.* https://www.gov.uk/government/statistics/hate-crime-england-and-wales-year-ending-march-2024/hate-crime-england-and-wales-year-ending-march-2024

Hughes, B. (1999). The constitution of impairment: Modernity and the aesthetic of oppression. *Disability & Society, 14*(2), 155–172.

Hughes, B. (2012). Fear, pity and disgust: Emotions and the non-disabled imaginary. In N. Watson, A. Roulstone & C. Thomas (Eds.), *Routledge handbook of disability studies* (1st ed., pp. 67–78). Routledge.

Imrie, R. F. (1996). *Disability and the city: International perspectives.* Paul Chapman.

Kelly, L. (1988). *Surviving sexual violence.* Polity Press.

Kitchin, R. (1998). "Out of place", "knowing one's place": Space, power and the exclusion of disabled people. *Disability & Society, 13*(3), 343–356. https://doi.org/10.1080/09687599826678

Leder, D. (1990). *The absent body.* University of Chicago Press.

Lenney, M., & Sercombe, H. (2002). 'Did you see that guy in the wheelchair down the pub?' Interactions across difference in a public place. *Disability & Society, 17*(1), 5–18. https://doi.org/10.1080/09687590120100093

Lewis, T. (2021, January 1). Working definition of ableism. *Talila Lewis.* Retrieved October 10 2024, from https://www.talilalewis.com/blog/january-2021-working-definition-of-ableism

Loja, E., Costa, M. E., Hughes, B., & Menezes, I. (2012). Disability, embodiment and ableism: Stories of resistance. *Disability & Society, 28*(2), 190–203. https://doi.org/10.1080/09687599.2012.705057

Mairs, N. (1996). *Carnal acts*. Beacon Press.

Mason-Bish, H. (2013). Conceptual issues in the construction of disability hate crime. In A. Roulstone & H. Mason-Bish (Eds.), *Disability, hate crime and violence* (pp. 11–24). Routledge.

McClimens, A., Partridge, N., & Sexton, E. (2014). How do people with learning disability experience the city centre? A Sheffield case study. *Health and Place, 28*, 14–21.

Morris, J. (1993). Feminism and disability. *Feminist Review, 43*(1), 57–70. https://doi.org/10.1057/fr.1993.4

Nario-Redmond, M. R., Kemerling, A. A., & Silverman, A. (2019). Hostile, benevolent, and ambivalent ableism: Contemporary manifestations. *Journal of Social Issues, 75*, 726–756. https://doi.org/10.1111/josi.12337

Nixon, J. (2009). Domestic violence and women with disabilities: Locating the issue on the periphery of social movements. *Disability & Society, 24*(1), 77–89. https://doi.org/10.1080/09687590802535709

Oliver, M. (1983). *Social work with disabled people*. Macmillan.

Oliver, M. (1990). *The politics of disablement*. Macmillan.

Oliver, M., & Barnes, C. (2012). *The new politics of disablement*. Palgrave.

Paterson, K., & Hughes, B. (1999). Disability studies and phenomenology: The carnal politics of everyday life. *Disability & Society, 14*(5), 597–610.

Pring, J. (2003). *Silent victims: The continuing failure to protect society's most vulnerable: The Longcare scandal*. Gibson Square.

Quarmby, K. (2011). *Scapegoat: Why we are failing disabled people*. London: Portobello.

Reeve, D. (2012). Psycho-emotional disablism: The missing link? In N. Watson, A. Roulstone & C. Thomas (Eds.), *Routledge handbook of disability studies* (1st ed., pp. 78–92). Routledge.

Rohrer, J. (2005). Toward a full-inclusion feminism: A feminist deployment of disability analysis. *Feminist Studies, 31*(1), 34–63.

RNIB. (2020). *How the lockdown is affecting blind and partially sighted people* (RNIB Briefing Paper). Retrieved October 10, 2024 from https://www.rnib.org.uk/living-with-sight-loss/independent-living/the-effect-of-lockdown-and-social-distancing/

Ryan, F. (2019). *Crippled: Austerity and the demonization of disabled people*. Verso Books.

Santos, A. C., & Santos, A. L. (2018). Yes, we fuck! Challenging the misfit sexual body through disabled women's narratives. *Sexualities, 21*(3), 303–318. https://doi.org/10.1177/1363460716688680

Shildrick, M. (1997). *Leaky bodies and boundaries: Feminism, postmodernism and (bio)ethics*. Routledge.

Thomas, C. (1999). *Female forms: Experiencing and understanding disability*. Open University Press.

Thomas, P. (2011). 'Mate crime': Ridicule, hostility and targeted attacks against disabled people. *Disability & Society, 26*(1), 107–111. https://doi.org/10. 1080/09687599.2011.532590

UPIAS. (1976). *Fundamental principles of disability*. Union of the Physically Impaired Against Segregation.

Vera-Gray, F. (2016). *Men's intrusion, women's embodiment: A critical analysis of street harassment*. Routledge.

Vera-Gray, F., & Kelly, L. (2020). Contested gendered space: Public sexual harassment and women's safety work. *International Journal of Comparative and Applied Criminal Justice, 44*(4), 265–275. https://doi.org/10.1080/ 01924036.2020.1732435

Walters, M. A. (2022). *Criminalising hate: Law as social justice liberalism*. Springer International Publishing AG.

Wayland, S., Newland, J., Gill-Atkinson, L., Vaughan, C., Emerson, E., & Llewellyn, G. (2020). I had every right to be there: Discriminatory acts towards young people with disabilities on public transport. *Disability & Society, 37*(2), 296–319. https://doi.org/10.1080/09687599. 2020.1822784

Whaley, K. (2016, January). Nobody catcalls the woman in the wheelchair. *The Establishment*. Retrieved October 10, 2024 from https://theestablishment. co/nobody-catcalls-the-woman-in-the-wheelchair-82a6e4517f79/index.html

Wilkin, D. (2020). *Disability hate crime: Experiences of everyday hostility on public transport*. Palgrave Macmillan.

Wolbring, G. (2008). The politics of ableism. *Development, 51*, 252–258. https://doi.org/10.1057/dev.2008.17

Zitzelsberger, H. (2005). (In)visibility: Accounts of embodiment of women with physical disabilities and differences. *Disability & Society, 20*(4), 389–403. https://doi.org/10.1080/09687590500086492

CHAPTER 3

Gathering Intersectional Narratives: A Feminist Approach to Disability Research

Abstract This chapter will outline the methodological approach of the project which was grounded in feminist disability studies. Offering a valuable perspective about retrieving 'dismissed voices and misrepresented experiences' (Garland-Thomson, 2005, p. 1557) the method involved developing a WordPress site where women could share their stories of unwanted and non-consensual touching. The chapter will discuss the practicalities of this approach and provide the reader with research reflections about using a narrative approach to gather and share the stories of participants in an ethical manner. The chapter also examines positionality and how the insider/outsider status of the author framed the research process. As a non-disabled researcher, the project was developed and carried out working closely with a visually impaired activist who advised on appropriate methodologies, language and was key in the sampling stage of the project. Overall, this chapter offers useful research perspectives on feminist disability research and practical tips on designing an ethical and inclusive project on often dismissed voices.

Keywords Feminist disability studies · Co-production · Positionality · Narrative methods · Intersectionality

© The Author(s), under exclusive license to Springer Nature
Switzerland AG 2025
H. Mason-Bish, *Disability, Gender, Bodies and Boundaries*, Palgrave
Hate Studies, https://doi.org/10.1007/978-3-031-85890-1_3

31

RESEARCH DESIGN BEGINNINGS

[We] invite strangers to enter our world, on our own terms, and to commence a dialogue on the basis of respect and equality. (Morris, 1996, p. 1)

Writing in the 1990s, disabled feminist Jenny Morris provided some guiding principles for non-disabled researchers as allies. These included the need to be active in thinking about the presence (or absence) of disabled researchers and working towards ensuring equality of opportunity in research and dissemination (Morris, 1992, p. 165). There must also be an attempt to recognise and challenge non-disabled attitudes towards disability. The research that we carry out must turn 'the spotlight on the oppressors' and make personal experiences of prejudice into political projects. As I am not a disabled woman, I followed these principles as the framework for the methodology used in this research and for every stage including planning, sampling, analysis and dissemination. This chapter will provide an honest account of this process and my personal reflections on positionality and ethical research. I reflect on how I asked myself unsettling questions in order to think critically about my role and my intentions in the pursuit of retrieving 'dismissed voices and misrepresented experiences (Garland-Thomson, 2005, p. 1557)'.

The inspiration for the research project came from the feminist history of sharing stories as a way to highlight and fight sexual violence. Since the 1970s, narratives have been used to create a rich repository of stories which have challenged cultural perceptions of violence against women. These provided the impetus for activism and changes in policy and practice. However, while campaigns such as the Me Too movement were focused on the sharing of stories, they have been criticised for foregrounding the voices of mostly white, non-disabled and heterosexual women (Phipps, 2020). Disabled women were routinely excluded from the Me Too movement and their stories overlooked (Flores, 2018; Lin & Yang, 2019). Disabled activists have sought to use online spaces to share experiences on their own terms. Hashtags such as #ableismtellsme function as a form of digital storytelling which encourage sharing, solidarity and can have an educative function (More, 2023). As the preceding chapters show, this project was inspired by the work of Amy Kavanagh, a blind campaigner and activist. Her online initiative, 'Just Ask, Don't Grab', had invited social media users to share their stories of being forcibly grabbed or touched when navigating public spaces. Amy's campaign therefore encouraged disabled men and women to talk about the unsolicited touching that happened to them, the access denials, the intrusive comments, the sexual assault. As I observed Amy's campaign develop, it was evident that disabled people would frequently express relief that these encounters were being talked about, a solidarity in not being the 'only one' and a hope that the stories would challenge stereotypes about them. Narratives had a positive energy in that they provided an outlet and sense of solidarity. However, they were sometimes contested spaces in that people would challenge the stories and demonstrate ableism in action by refuting or denying the harm caused.

Drawing on these approaches, the focus of this research was to explore the ways that disabled women experience non-consensual touching when out in public places. It had these objectives:

- To explore how disabled women experience touching in public and how this might be intrusive; unwanted or non-consensual.
- To explore whether or not it impacts on or limits the freedom of movement that disabled women have and what measures they might take to avoid it.
- To begin to draw out the deeper intersectional nature of these experiences and the impact this might have on their identity.

A commitment to the lived and living experiences is at the heart of much feminist disability work as it allows a deeper understanding of the way that women attach meaning to the behaviours that happen to them. It can also move away from individualised encounters and points towards broader structures and mechanisms of power and discrimination. With that in mind, a qualitative, phenomenological approach was adopted. In her work on men's stranger intrusions, Fiona Vera-Gray outlines the case for feminist phenomenological methodologies as allowing us to illuminate assumptions, particularly in everyday behaviours that are often deemed trivial (Vera-Gray, 2017, p. 29). This is especially relevant given the focus of much work on violence against women which has looked at prevalence or which has concentrated on behaviours deemed criminal in law. Writing in the 1990s, Jenny Morris observed that disability activism had pushed for the social model and this meant critiquing the way that society disables people. She emphasised the need to embrace individual experiences (Morris, 1992).

STORYTELLING AND NARRATIVE RETRIEVAL

As previous chapters have demonstrated, there has only been a very small amount of academic research focusing on disabled women and their public experiences of intrusive touching. Starting from this basis, I wanted to design a project that was easy for people to participate in and one that did not demand too much of their time. Burch (2024) points to the way that online methodologies enhance opportunities for disabled people to participate in research. This is because they are cost effective, more accessible and allow contribution at times that suit them and their lives. Thinking about the emotional labour required and the possibility for trauma, I decided that the best way would be to gather stories using an online WordPress site where participants could send their narrative experiences and be free to write as much or as little as they wished. They would be given a loose structure and framework which provided guidance but allowed them to tell their stories in the most open way possible. They would also have guidance on the sorts of topic that they might like to cover:

'where/when the incident happened.
how it felt at the time
how you reacted and what followed from it.
how this incident fits within the broader spectrum of your experience of non-consensual touching.
the impact this has had on you longer term.
if you wish, share some information about yourself and your identity such as age; disability; race; gender identity'.

This design centred a commitment to 'narrative retrieval' and the need to hear stories of 'distinct perspectives on sexuality, reproductive issues, appearance biases, and other shared struggles' (Garland-Thomson, 2005, p. 1560). In their work on narrative in disability studies, Smith and Sparkes speak of the difference between a story analyst and a story-telling approach (2008). In the former, an analysis of a story allows scrutiny and theoretical development but in the latter, the story itself is analytical. When people tell their stories, they are employing 'analytic techniques to interpret their worlds' (p. 21). Furthermore, collective stories have the power to transform discourse and challenge stereotypes. This is particularly the case for disability studies research as Ahlvik-Harju explains:

> Life stories about corporeal difference have the power to point at the intricate connections between subjective experience and the cultural narrative and exemplify how narratives about the 'normal body' damages and hurts people embodying something else. (Ahlvik-Harju, 2016, p. 226)

My intention at the design stage was that when it came to analysing responses, I would be thinking about how the process of sharing the stories was part of their conceptualisation, where they would be interpreting their world. Storytelling produces rather than reflects reality (Lockwood & Scott, 2023, p. 216). The guiding questions would encourage the participants to think of experiences within the broader framework of their lives, as well as the specific detail of individual occurrences. As Jackson and Scott (2023) describe, this is because they are often sense-making activities which include explanations or theorisations of the past—'this happened because'. In terms of feminist disability studies, this type of storytelling and narrative sharing has particular significance. Simplican talks of this in relation to disabled women:

> Because ableism and sexism intersect to construct disabled women as asexual, miserable and powerless, life-writing is especially useful because it empowers disabled women to tell their own stories that counter sexual and ableist marginalisation. (Simplican, 2017, p. 48)

As the research progressed it became clear that the process of telling stories was indeed cathartic, with some participants expressing their anger and frustration when thinking back on intrusive encounters. Many also provided their broader reflections on the ableism and sexism that framed their experiences and what needed to change. Stories sometimes included a discussion about the participants' sense of self and how their gender and disability framed their daily encounters. The process of narrative retrieval therefore included this type of sense-making activity which helped to understand broader aspects of ableism.

Positionality, Ethics and Allyship

Taking up space in advocacy for a marginalized group is a privilege; one that you can wield to make the public sphere more inclusive or one you can use to center yourself. Ally-ship requires you to do the former, anything else is a performance. (Barbarin, 2018)

Disability activist Imani Barbarin's principles for allyship provide an excellent guide for non-disabled people negotiating their role in disability research. As a scholar of hate crime and victimisation, my privileged positionality has often been concerning to me and something that I have spent the best part of twenty years thinking about and navigating. As a white, heterosexual and non-disabled woman, I occupy a position of privilege. I am an academic with a permanent contract at a University and so have the time and resources to undertake research. And yet I have also experienced the daily sexist intrusions that came to form part of the stories that my participants told. I take on the repertoire of safety measures, so common to many women, when I leave the house. This familiarity presents an entry point to the research but always from the position that it is a different experience. Barnes and Mercer (1997) wrote about the role of non-disabled people in disability research and warned against being an 'academic tourist' and producing inauthentic research. They point out that research on disabled people has frequently been exploitative rather than liberating and only served to maintain unequal power relations. In this vein, I was cautious about taking on narratives of empowerment. As a non-disabled researcher it is not appropriate for me to speak of empowering the participants in my research because that plays into a stereotype of disabled people as passive and lacking in agency. I am not 'giving them a voice' but rather using my research as a vehicle in which they can share their voice and experiences. It was important to also note that the work was ontologically grounded in the social model of disability. This means that the aims and objectives outlined above were framed around identifying the ableist and sexist nature of intrusive behaviours and how they impacted on the disabled participant. My positionality in this regard meant avoiding suggestions that the disability was the cause of the unwanted touching. Writers in feminist disability studies have implored non-disabled feminists to 'lend their strength to the naming of women's experiences within any analysis of disability' (Lloyd, 1992,

p. 219). Writing in 2013, disability scholar and activist Susie Balderston said that feminist researchers:

> after conceiving of the extent and patterns of heterogeneous violence against women, must now be called to struggle against the significant oppressions and harms perpetrated against disabled and Deaf women. (Balderston, 2013, pp. 18–19)

Feminist academics should not expect disabled women to bear the burden of researching traumatic violence committed against them, instead they should work alongside them, being cognisant of their positionality. Susie died at the end of 2023 and we were in touch not long before where we talked about this project. Her work remains my guidance in being an appropriate ally.

I knew that I needed the project to be a co-production with an experienced disability activist or researcher. Burch (2024) speaks of participatory research in disability studies and a commitment not just to collaboration but also co-creation. This should be about research design, but also the ways of working, types of issues and the knowledge that is being developed (Burch, 2024, p. 3938). As the inspiration for the research, in the preliminary stages I had been in contact with Amy Kavanagh. She agreed to work with me in developing the project by being a consultant, paid for by my own internal research allowance. Our initial discussions were very much focused on the kind of project we wanted to create—how we wanted participants to feel, thinking about their emotional wellbeing and the overall purpose of the project. Once the research began we checked in regularly as I shared the data with Amy and the key findings. She also advised on appropriate methodologies including language. Her networking and the validity that she gave to the project was also key in the sampling stages. I am well aware that I had to live up to the expectations of participants in terms of what her endorsement suggested. Without Amy, this study would not have been possible. Once we launched the project we got a lot of media attention and requests for interviews and Op-Ed pieces. In most cases we did these jointly, with Amy as the main voice or lead writer to ensure the continuation of this approach. I continue to pass along paid opportunities which do not meet with this commitment to allyship.

The process of gaining ethical approval meant ensuring, as much as possible, that participants were not harmed in the process of sharing their stories. I found that there was also a quandary here in terms of concerns raised by my ethics committee. The ethics process requires thinking about the vulnerability of research participants as disabled women. It is entirely appropriate to consider the risks faced by participants, particularly in relation to trauma and emotional harm. Yet the positioning of disabled women as inherently vulnerable is problematic, particularly if it means that research embracing their experiences is avoided. As Love and McDonnell (2024, p. 6) suggest, research can open up the space to 'subvert and resist' stigmas which assume vulnerability. Reflecting back on the principles for allies in disability research that Jenny Morris proposed, I was committed to the idea that studies should work to highlight discriminatory and abusive practices and give 'expression to the anger, pain and hurt resulting from such experiences' (Morris, 1992, p. 165). An interesting observation in the submissions was how many participants expressed gratitude for the research being carried out. Often a 'thank goodness someone is talking about it'. Watharow and Wayland express that it is in thinking about empowerment and how narrative conversations are enabled that it can embolden 'participants to make informed choices and to tell their stories, in their own way, they also affirm the subject of study' (2022, p. 3).

Appropriate allyship is an ongoing process of learning and adaptation that I continue to reflect upon and there are some tensions in positionality that are not resolved for me. The topic itself and the stories that follow include unpleasant, abusive and hostile behaviours towards disabled women. Jenny Morris explained that sometimes the non-disabled feminist 'focus on the "double disadvantage" of disability and sexism can only feed into the negative attitudes of those "feeling sorry" for us' (Morris, 1996, p. 4). In talking about victimisation, my research may contribute to a narrative that invites people to pity disabled women. It is hoped though that in being a conduit for the stories of participants I can assist in amplifying their voices and adding to the limited literature in this area. Furthermore, I have adopted a tone in framing the stories that allows for a critical examination of the ableist and sexist assumptions that cause unwanted intrusions. In short, this book uses the lived experiences to shine a spotlight back on the discriminatory causes and practices rather than the victimisation itself. A further contentious issue is that academic publishing is embedded within power structures, open mainly to scholars who are more likely to be in permanent positions (see Brown & Leigh, 2020). To navigate these dilemmas, Phipps

(2016) suggests a careful reflection on what platforms are appropriate, particularly thinking about the line between talking about your work and 'ventriloquising other people's experiences'. For this reason, the three chapters that follow feature many stories of participants in full, as they were written and intended to be read.

SAMPLING STRATEGIES

Having decided upon a method by which to gather the stories, I designed the WordPress site and then employed the services of an expert in disability accessibility in website design. This was to ensure that the layout, font size and general appearance were accessible to participants with a broad range of impairments. Other information on the site included sample stories, links to resources if additional help was required and a participant information sheet. In the design it was key that the stories of the participants would have central focus and as these were received they were uploaded onto the homepage. I would only change the names to a pseudonym in order to keep the integrity of the way they were written and expressed. The site also included a link to Amy Kavanagh's website and Just Ask, Don't Grab campaign. It was important to convey that this was a co-creation and to create confidence in participants that stories would be handled sensitively. She was my guide in terms of navigating respectful, participatory research.

In terms of sampling decisions, the first that I had to make was about whose stories I wanted to gather in terms of impairment and gender identity. Disabled men also experience unwanted touching and there is certainly an important piece of work to be done in broadening the focus of ableist intrusions to include them. However, my entry point had been from a feminist disability studies perspective and embracing intersectional experiences, so it was women that I wanted to hear from. Early on in the sampling discussions, Amy and I had shared our trans-inclusive approach to feminism and wanted to signpost this to potential contributors. Non-binary people may present as femme and continue to be underrepresented in research. It is recognised that a limitation of this study is that non-binary voices could have been recruited with more careful targeting of the sampling process as only a few identified as such in the stories provided. In order to provide an intersectional approach that is respectful of different experiences of gender identity and disability, a further study is required which focuses on people who identify as disabled non-binary. The limited narratives provided for this study have been included at various points in this book, but the main analysis relates to people who said they were disabled women. I did not want to be impairment specific and so merely invited 'disabled women and non-binary people'. As well as a link to Amy's blog and campaign I also linked to the Bronwyn Berg article about being pushed in her wheelchair and Kiruma Stamell's (2016) piece about how people with dwarfism face ridicule. The site introduced the research by saying:

> 'As part of a research project that I am conducting at the University of Sussex, I am looking for contributions from disabled women and non-binary people who have experienced non-consensual touching from strangers in public spaces. These might be the unwanted 'helping hand' of a stranger who touches you. They might be gentle or more forceful in nature. They might escalate when you respond and end in hostility or violence. They might also be in the form of sexual violence or harassment.
>
> The common theme is that they often involve some form of physical touch and they are non-consensual. Say as much or as little as you wish.'

The strategy in terms of sampling was to employ my networks and those of Amy and other social media influencers to promote the project. As Fiona Vera-Gray notes, a challenge in this kind of research is to be careful about naming the behaviour that you might want to capture because women will self exclude if they don't define it in the terms you propose (Vera-Gray, 2017, p. 30). We devised a series of simple tweets explaining that we were looking for stories on non-consensual touching of disabled women and non-binary people. It followed with a few examples 'we are looking for stories. These might be the unwanted "helping hand" of a stranger who touches you. They might be gentle or more forceful in nature. They might also be in the form of sexual violence or harassment'. All linked through to the website which had further information describing the continuum of behaviours we hoped to capture:

> 'Are you a disabled woman or non-binary person who has experienced non-consensual touching in a public place?
>
> Have you been grabbed; pushed; tapped; pulled or forcibly 'helped'?
>
> Have you experienced intrusive behaviour or questions from strangers?'

The sampling strategy was successful in that it led to 75 stories being received in the first 6 weeks of launch due mainly to social media attention and being retweeted and endorsed by some high profile activists including Paralympian Dame Tanni Grey-Thompson. We were invited onto BBC radio 4's Woman's Hour and asked to write for the Metro, the Independent and Huffington Post. These all served to increase the attention paid to the project and the stories coming in. Although we did not officially close the submissions, after three months or so numbers had started to decline with a total of 80 stories being received.

WHICH STORIES ARE TOLD

The people who shared their stories with the project were understandably a self selecting sample who had heard about the project via the Tweets shared online. There is likely to be bias towards disabled people who have access to technology and who are regular users of social media. Followers of Amy Kavanagh's activism who might be familiar with her campaign are more likely to respond because of this shared experience. This has repercussions in terms of age, with the demographic potentially being younger. That said, we did use other means by way of coverage on local radio stations and in national newspapers and magazines to broaden recruitment. Despite a commitment to uncovering the lost and dismissed voices that guide principles of feminist disability studies, it is recognised that the sample in this study is not representative. However, the aim of the project had been to gather experiences of everyday hostility and unwanted touching, a previously underexplored area. The stories thus enabled the sketching out of a concept of ableist intrusions and to give a platform to people who are usually overlooked.

Due to the open nature of the stories we requested, we do not have detailed demographic data about the participants but instead asked them to comment on other aspects of their identity which they deemed to be relevant or wanted to share. This was a deliberate choice so as not to over burden participants with requests for information when they were already sharing sensitive and troubling information. In that sense, self-categorisation is seen to be an exercise of power and autonomy which recognises their ownership of their identity (Crenshaw, 1991). Through their own narratives and descriptions they are identifying what elements might be important to the story they are telling. However, it means that I cannot assert that the study challenges the charge of white privilege that is often directed towards disability studies. Amongst our participants around 40% indicated that they had a visual impairment and used an assistance dog or white cane and around 40% were wheelchair users. This is perhaps unsurprising given that mobility aids come to form part of how people view disability. Frequently, intrusions were focused specifically on the mobility aid as part of the unwanted touching. A further 10% of participants reported using a stick or cane to assist with walking and did not necessarily list a specific impairment. Others detailed having a skin condition; cerebral palsy; autism and/or dyspraxia, dwarfism or ME. The role of the mobility aid as a visual identifier of disability and also the target of unwanted touching became a central aspect of the research. Not only was it the way that strangers identified someone as disabled, it also became the focal point of unwanted intrusion and fed into the way that disabled women did safety work. For example, participants spoke about altering their mobility aid, leaving it at home or taking difficult routes to avoid being touched. They also reflected on the different nature of intrusions depending on the mobility aid being used. It also was a site of assessment of competence, meaning that people would challenge their skill and use it when in public. It was the gateway to intrusive questions and remarks. People also documented their immediate responses to being touched and the significant emotion work that was done to keep themselves safe. In all, the stories provided a brief but rich insight into the lived experiences of disabled women as they negotiate public spaces.

ANALYSIS OF FINDINGS

The stories were analysed using a thematic coding framework. At the outset I had approached the research with the aim of finding out what was happening on an everyday basis for disabled women. This meant that I anticipated coding firstly in a fairly descriptive way to identify what was happening. Using the computer software package MaxQDA I firstly coded each story by identifying the impairment described and the nature of unwanted touching. This open coding then was used to identify more selective themes. It became clear quite quickly that the nature of the intrusion was connected with the mobility aid as a visible symbol of disability. It was also something that participants mentioned in their self-guided descriptions of themselves. Similarly, the words used to describe the touching also made up the themes in point 2 below. Codes 3 and 5 related to the responses and impacts of touching as they were relayed in the immediate aftermath of intrusion and on reflection. Codes 4, 6 and 7 emerged after selective coding which meant refining and thinking about the bigger picture of what was going on. The 7 themes with numerous sub-themes are detailed below:

Theme	Sub themes
1. Impairment	1.1 Skin Condition 1.2 Vocal 1.3 Cerebral Palsy 1.4 Deaf 1.5 Uses Stick/Cane 1.6 Autism 1.7 Wheelchair User 1.8 Visual Impairment 1.9 Dwarfism 1.10 ME
2. Nature of touching	2.1 Spitting 2.2 Personal Questions/insults 2.3 Shouting 2.4 Being leant on 2.5 Mobility aid touched/pushed 2.6 Reference to multiple previous incidents 2.7 Being cornered/forced into a room 2.8 Sexual assault 2.9 Being lifted 2.10 Pushing or grabbing 2.11 Perpetrator reflections
3. Responses to being touched	3.1 Fear of escalation/not knowing what might happen 3.2 Feelings/emotional response 3.2.1 Powerlessness 3.2.2 Embarrassment 3.2.3 Confusion 3.2.4 Anger 3.3 Either no response/ polite/muted 3.4 Hitting back 3.5 Shouting/ screaming
4. Motivations of perpetrators	4.1 People assume help is needed 4.1.1 being treated like a child 4.1.2 being a woman. 4.2 disability hierarchies 4.2.1 being treated like an inconvenience 4.2.2 age 4.3 Perpetrator responses 4.3.1 mocking/laughing 4.3.2 only trying to help 4.3.3 anger/aggression
5. Impacts	5.1 Defensiveness 5.2 physical injury/pain 5.3 emotional responses 5.3.1 loss of confidence 5.3.2 violation 5.3.3 anxiety/nervousness 5.4 change of daily life 5.4.1 making personality smaller 5.4.2 change of mobility aid 5.4.3 not being able to work
6. Hopes for change	6.1 greater understanding of consent 6.2 to be treated like a human being 6.3 recognition of intersectionality 6.4 being allowed to move through the world
7. Broader reflections	7.1 being treated like an object 7.2 being a woman in public 7.3 a common experience 7.4 shifting blame 7.5 it could have been worse 7.6 being ignored/silenced

As with any coding framework the multiple codes provide both descriptive and more analytical tools which speak to the richness of the stories that were told. Quite quickly it became clear that Fiona Vera-Gray's concept of intrusions was a better categorisation than unwanted touching. This was because a common description of the behaviours encountered was of questions and personal insults which were not about touch specifically. Intrusion 'is used here to refer to the deliberate act of putting oneself into a place or situation where one is uninvited, with disruptive effect (Vera-Gray, 2017, p. 11)'. Across the contributions, the participants talked of the lived experience of unwanted intrusion in complex ways. Many discussed how their disabled body was viewed by a society which prioritises able-bodied lives and how their gender and disability contributed to an entitlement of people to intrude. The ableist intrusion concept which will be developed in the subsequent chapters is therefore a descriptive tool but also an analytical one. Other unexpected themes emerged such as the role of emotion work which participants spoke of in some detail. While they expressed anger, frustration and sadness at being touched, they would often hide their reactions so as not to provoke further hostility or intrusion upon them. Although in a project like this there is a necessary attempt to synergise key themes and similarities, it is important to note that each contributor detailed their own individual reactions which speak to their agency, assertion and right to move in public without being touched. What is drawn from analysis is the shared ontologies of ableism and sexism that define daily interactions. In the next three chapters, many of the stories are shared in full or at some length in order to retain the authenticity and context in which they were intended to be read.

Research Reflections

Gathering the stories of disabled women allowed me to sketch out a typology of behaviours that many experienced on a regular basis. Using a feminist disability studies approach meant that the embodied lives of participants were the focal point of the research. This challenges the notion of the female, disabled body as 'less than' by allowing women to speak their truth about how their bodies are perceived and touched by strangers in public places. Their perceptions about motivation, harm and impacts are prioritised. It is also a political project, with the aim of highlighting unwanted behaviours to the wider public as evidenced in the media work undertaken and the principle of leaving the stories online as a community document. However, there are elements of the research that continue to be challenging. As a non-disabled woman, a partial outsider, I 'controlled' the direction of the research. I am writing the book, receiving academic attention for the labours and words of others (Phipps, 2016). It is hoped that in paying heed to the words of Jenny Morris in terms of being a respectful ally, the work can contribute to greater understanding of the embodied lives of disabled women and the impact of unwanted touching and intrusions on their lives. The next chapter will sketch out the details about the nature and scope of ableist intrusions using the words of the women who contributed.

REFERENCES

Ahlvik-Harju, C. (2016). Disturbing bodies—Reimagining comforting narratives of embodiment through feminist disability studies. *Scandinavian Journal of Disability Research, 18*(3), 222–233. https://doi.org/10.1080/15017419.2015.1063545

Balderston, S. (2013). Victimised again? Intersectionality and injustice in disabled women's lives after hate crime and rape. In M. Texler Segal, & V. Demos (Eds.), *Gendered perspectives on conflict and violence: Part A*. Advances in Gender Research, Volume 18A (pp. 17–51). Emerald Group Publishing Ltd.

Barbarin, I. (2018). Disabled people have an ally problem: They need to stop talking for us. *Crutches and Spice*. Retrieved October 11, 2024, from https://crutchesandspice.com/2018/05/15/disabled-people-have-an-ally-problem-they-need-to-stop-talking-for-us/

Barnes, C., & Mercer, G. (1997). Breaking the mould? An introduction to doing disability research. In C. Barnes & G. Mercer (Eds.), *Doing disability research* (pp. 1–14). Disability Press.

Brown, N., & Leigh, J. (Eds.). (2020). *Ableism in academia: Theorising experiences of disabilities and chronic illnesses in higher education*. UCL Press. https://doi.org/10.14324/111.9781787354975

Burch, L. (2024). Working "with" not "on" disabled people: The role of hate crime research within the community. *Journal of Interpersonal Violence, 39*(17–18), 3932–3953. https://doi.org/10.1177/08862605241260005

Crenshaw, K. (1991, July). Mapping the margins: Intersectionality, identity politics, and violence against women of color. *Stanford Law Review, 43*(6), 1241–1299.

Flores, E. (2018). The #MeToo movement hasn't been inclusive of the disability community. *Teen Vogue*. Retrieved October 11, 2024 from https://www.teenvogue.com/story/the-metoo-movement-hasnt-been-inclusive-of-the-disability-community

Garland-Thomson, R. (2005). Feminist disability studies: A review of essays. *Signs, 30*(2), 1557–1587.

Jackson, S., & Scott, S. (2023). Storytelling, sociology and sexuality: Ken Plummer's humanist narrative analysis. *Sexualities, 26*(4), 476–485. https://doi.org/10.1177/13634607231169003

Lin, Z., & Yang, L. (2019). 'Me too!': Individual empowerment of disabled women in the #MeToo movement in China. *Disability & Society, 34*(5), 842–847. https://doi.org/10.1080/09687599.2019.1596608

Lloyd, M. (1992). Does she boil eggs? Towards a feminist model of disability. *Disability, Handicap & Society, 7*(3), 207–221. https://doi.org/10.1080/02674649266780231

Lockwood, N., & Scott, S. (2023). Saying something with nothing: Refusal, avoidance and resistance in participant non-response. *Methodological Innovations, 16*(2), 215–225. https://doi.org/10.1177/20597991231179390

Love, G., & McDonnell, L. (2024). Presence as politics in qualitative research ethics: Feminist engagements with "risk" and vulnerability. *Qualitative Inquiry.* https://doi.org/10.1177/10778004241256141

More, R. (2023). Storying ableism: Proposing a feminist intersectional approach to linking theory and digital activism. *Feminist Theory, 25*(3), 322–337. https://doi.org/10.1177/14647001231173242

Morris, J. (1992). Personal and political: A feminist perspective on researching physical disability. *Disability, Handicap & Society, 7*, 157–166.

Morris, J. (1996). *Encounters with strangers: Feminism and disability.* The Women's Press.

Phipps, A. (2016). *Responsible self-promotion: negotiating the relationships between self and other, myself and 'my' work.* Retrieved October 10, 2024 from https://phipps.space/2016/02/18/responsible-self-promotion/

Phipps, A. (2020). *Me, not you: The trouble with mainstream feminism.* Manchester University Press.

Simplican, S. C. (2017). Feminist disability studies as methodology: Life-writing and the abled/disabled binary. *Feminist Review, 115*(1), 46–60.

Smith, B., & Sparkes, A. C. (2008). Narrative and its potential contribution to disability studies. *Disability & Society, 23*(1), 17–28. https://doi.org/10.1080/09687590701725542

Stamell, K. (2016, March 29). *People with dwarfism deserve respect—Not ridicule.* Retrieved 10 October, 2024 from https://www.theguardian.com/commentisfree/2016/mar/29/people-dwarfism-deserve-respect

Vera-Gray, F. (2018). *The right amount of panic: How women trade freedom for safety in public.* Policy Press.

Vera-Gray, F. (2017). *Men's intrusion, women's embodiment: A critical analysis of street harassment.* Routledge.

Watharow, A., & Wayland, S. (2022). Making qualitative research inclusive: Methodological insights in disability research. *International Journal of Qualitative Methods, 21*. https://doi.org/10.1177/16094069221095316

CHAPTER 4

Outlining Ableist Intrusions

Abstract This chapter details the experiences of disabled women and the daily intrusions that happen to them. The concept of ableist intrusions is developed to demonstrate how disabled women experience a range of incidents, from intrusive comments to physical violence and sexual assault. The chapter includes a discussion of how these experiences are embodied and how disabled women typically feel objectified and infantilised by what happens to them. The chapter will also situate these unwanted intrusions within the wider context of disability stereotypes to illustrate how intrusions are manifestations of a broader societal attitude towards disability, which reinforces ableist norms and values. Using the words of participants in the research project to evidence this point, the chapter discusses the role of the mobility aid as a visible symbol of disability, which frequently triggers ableist intrusions. The overall goal of the chapter is to outline a typology of behaviours that constitute ableist intrusion and to reveal new insights on the socio-cultural factors that are conducive to such encounters.

Keywords Ableist intrusions · Embodiment · Disabled stereotypes · Mobility aid · Sexual assault

© The Author(s), under exclusive license to Springer Nature
Switzerland AG 2025
H. Mason-Bish, *Disability, Gender, Bodies and Boundaries*, Palgrave
Hate Studies, https://doi.org/10.1007/978-3-031-85890-1_4

47

The Push, Grab and Lift

I lost my central vision almost two years ago and have been using a white cane since then. Since I began using the cane, I have been grabbed by strangers more times than I can possibly count. Almost every time I leave my apartment, at least one person will touch me without consent to try to move me wherever they think I want to go. I hate being touched, and it makes me incredibly anxious to know that strangers feel free to touch me without permission. When it happens, I feel threatened, humiliated, and furious. I have a tendency to freeze in these situations, but I always feel worse afterwards if I didn't stand up for myself, so I am working on being prepared to snap at people who put their hands on me.

One incident in particular stands out to me. I was at the national NFB convention, which was very crowded, so I was already feeling tense. I got into an elevator full of people, and a man standing behind me grabbed both of my shoulders to move me. I pulled his hands away and told him to keep his hands off of me. He just told me to calm down. I moved toward the buttons to find the one for my floor, and he grabbed my arm again. I yelled, "What did I just tell you?" A man near the back of the elevator joked, "You can touch me if you want." Everyone laughed. As I got off the elevator, a couple of people yelled comments about how I was getting upset over nothing. I'll never forget how angry and hopeless I felt, having an elevator full of people side with a man who touched me without consent and laugh at me for trying to defend myself, and not being able to do a thing about it. I'll never forget the realization that I can expect everyone to laugh at me and no one to support me when I am harassed in public. There is nothing I can do to force people to see me as a human being and respect my boundaries. It is hell.

Alyssa provided a vivid description of the nature of unwanted intrusions that she experiences as a disabled woman. Her words speak to the way that people feel entitled to touch her and to mock and humiliate her when she attempts to establish her boundaries. In that moment she describes not being treated as a human being and the sense of anger and frustration that this evokes. She also speaks of a very common description, articulated by almost all participants in this study, that intrusive behaviours are a frequent occurrence when moving through public space as a disabled woman. Tai, a wheelchair user, provided a number of examples but described these as just the 'tip of the iceberg' as it happened with 'alarming regularity'. The routine nature with which incidents occur can have significant consequences for individuals' expectations relating to how they negotiate public space. Kerry notes that her life is 'filled with unexpected violations' where even mundane activities become complicated due to the 'extreme behaviour' of members of the public.

Alyssa's account of having her shoulders grabbed by a man who wanted to move her out of the way forms one of the most common types of physical intrusion that participants frequently described. Pushing or grabbing was described as happening for two reasons. First, because the disabled person was 'in the way' and second, to move them under the guise of assuming that they need help. Taking the first reason as a starting point, Denise, who works with a guide dog and previously was a white cane user, describes the continuum of these instances:

Being pushed from behind whilst I am taking a split second to navigate a step or doorway because they think I need help moving forwards. This often ends up with me falling. I have been pushed off buses and trains.

Being pulled when I've asked for directions or an orientation point such as a counter.

Being forced to do something such as having my hand grabbed when I have my freedom pass in it and forcibly placed on the card reader.

A man behind me grabbed the tops of both of my arms and said "I want to get on the train" and forced me out of the way, still holding on. I thought I was being pushed under the train.

These constant intrusions against individuals' bodily autonomy mean that disabled women become annoying objects, an inconvenience to the non-disabled priority in public space. It is further evidenced by the way that participants described how people would grab them without speaking or asking them first. June described being pushed and pulled by people in order to be shown the way, rather than people using words of assistance. The physicality of exchanges is illustrative of how disabled women are seen as 'things' that are 'out of place' or are infantalised and not able to move in public space without assistance. In other contexts, participants spoke of feeling infantalised, both through the tone in which non-disabled people spoke to them, as well as how they were handled non-consensually by those attempting to 'help'. Their bodies may be noticed, but their 'capacities, lives and desires [remain] unseen' (Zitzelsberger, 2005, p. 394). These examples depicted an able-bodied entitlement through which disabled women are simply moved out of the way. June provided further detail of such an incident at a bus stop:

> I was waiting at a bus stop. I had reached one foot forward to check my position relative to the curb. A young woman behind me ran up and grabbed my right elbow in what she thought was her attempt to keep me from going into the street. I have been physically attacked by someone who used that ploy and my instinctive reaction when grabbed is to give a hard elbow check to the person. I did this to the young woman and yelled something I don't recall. We were both horribly embarrassed, but she did not understand why doing this was not a good idea and that I actually did know exactly where I was and what I was doing.

June's account demonstrates a number of features of ableist intrusion which are about being grabbed or pushed. She details the sudden and interrupting nature with which they can occur, in a moment when she was focused on checking her own position and safety. She is grabbed, jolted into an unsafe position and unsure of the motivation of the person grabbing her. Such encounters privilege the anxiety of the person doing the grabbing—who might be assuming that help is required—but they also force the disabled person into assessing what their intention is. In this situation, June elbows them back as a clear sign that help is not required. Her physical reaction seems to carry more weight than a verbal one.

In addition to grabbing and pushing, participants described other intrusions including being leant on or lifted. Anje has chronic pain and periods of weakness where she might collapse. She described how whenever she has a pain episode, people would suddenly grab her, rub her back or try to sit her up. Anje went on to detail a particular incident when she had fallen over at a tech rehearsal for a play she was in:

> All of a sudden, about 30 people rushed in around me, and every available space had hands on me. My stage manager even tried to forcefully pull me up, twisting my back and causing me to scream out in pain. A stranger I didn't know kept rubbing my back even after everyone else backed off, and I wanted to just rip her hand off.

Then, when I had to make it into a car, a couple well-meaning friends just picked me up. When I said I could get there once we were down the steps, they didn't put me down, and physically placed me in the car themselves. It was uncomfortable and demeaning.

As with June's example, Anje describes how the physical touching and lifting happens without request for consent. Strangers are touching her during a moment of vulnerability in extremely intimate ways which led her to feel pain and that she was being demeaned. In cases of being picked up or lifted, other participants felt that people were making an assessment of them as weak and that the public were feeling an anxiety in seeing a body that was out of control. AJ, a woman with dwarfism, talked about being put on someone's shoulders at a music festival, again without permission and with force. She went on to list other examples such as people putting their hands on her back or arm to escort her on public transport or passengers putting luggage in overhead storage without asking. The lack of conversation before the intrusion was almost ubiquitous. The disabled participants in this study were not given the opportunity to refuse the touching and when a verbal exchange did happen it was presented not as a question but as an instruction.

Mobility Aid Intrusions

Many participants in the study used a mobility aid. Wheelchairs, white canes and assistance dogs are not just 'visual signifiers' of disability, they can become the focal point of ableist intrusions (Calder-Dawe et al., 2019; Worth, 2013). In this study, wheelchair users more commonly noted people using them to lean on or to hang objects from. Sally discusses people using her wheelchair as a 'leaning post' and that it would be held onto in busy public transport or crowds. Others experienced their wheelchair being pushed without their consent, being moved around buildings or put out of the way. Participants could also discern differences specifically related to which aid they were using. Sally explains:

I'm an ambulatory wheelchair user, and my main mobility aid is an electric bike. When I use a wheelchair it is a rigid manual with a smartdrive. This means I'm mobile on my own, without needing "help" from people to push me. It also means I transition a lot from wheelchair use to non wheelchair use. When I'm using a bike noone touches me. Noone tries to 'help' me – even when it would genuinely be helpful! When I'm a wheelchair user it's constant. It is one of the many things that makes wheelchair use very stressful.

Yasmin, a wheelchair user for 12 years, describes how her experiences of non-consensual touching were often focused on her mobility aid:

> It ranges from people pushing me without asking and with no warning, which has not only been rude but dangerous, as I have nearly lost my balance and fallen forward out of my chair to people leaning on my chair or touching it without my permission... The presumption that I need help all the time is bad enough but to just push a person without even asking assumes that I am a charity case and someone to be rescued who obviously need assistance constantly to get around. How do people think I manage on a daily basis? It's such an instinctive reaction.

Yasmin's story illustrates how disabled women are not only reduced to 'things' but can in fact be subjected to an additional precarity which puts their health at risk. This constant perilous state in which disabled people are seen to occupy leads to an almost 'need' to react on behalf of strangers. This can be described as an ableist anxiety where people feel that they have to 'do something' when they encounter a visibly disabled person. Aside from forced offers of 'help' or moving Yasmin out of the way as an inconvenience, she also talks about 'jokes' that punctuate her day:

> I have had some people be apologetic when I respond to them but they tend to then follow it quickly with a justification, "oh i was only trying to help" or "you looked like you were struggling" or they will just shrug and look bemused as if I am being so ungrateful. It's really tiring and I find dealing with people harder than the disability itself. I seem to have got over it but it seems others find disability so confronting that they feel they need to react in some way either by their behaviour or even making some kind of comment about the chair. Sometimes you just want a day off.

> I get probably daily comments about the way I move around to the usual "jokes" directed at wheelchair users, "oh you should get a licence for that", "oh don't drink and drive" etc which I find so boring as I've heard it probably 400 times or more. I think people are so awkward about disability and feel they need to say something when "hello" will suffice.

Literature on street harassment has detailed the way that being a woman in public is to become used to intrusive 'humorous' comments. These cover a broad spectrum including jokes about appearance, being asked to 'smile' and other 'verbal ejaculations' (Gardner, 1995; Laniya, 2005). However for disabled women, these attempts at humour are perceived as coming from a combination of privilege, awkwardness and a need to comment on the presence of the disabled person in public space. Butler and Bowlby (1997) detail the fact that only those whose bodies conform to acceptable standards can have a physical presence in a public space without comment or remarks (p. 419). It is evident that the jokes are drawing on well-rehearsed, patronising scripts of women being bad drivers and not possessing the skill required to control vehicles appropriately.

A further element of the focus on mobility aids is the extent to which disabled women were assumed not to know about their own access needs. Viv described this in a list of intrusive behaviours she was very familiar with:

> Is it a carer deciding what you are or aren't going to eat. Is it when in a queue the person standing with you is asked what your order is although you are the adult!, is it when a nurse decides that you don't need continence care so refuses to assist, thus leaving you in distress, is it when someone you have never spoken to before in a social environment wants to know 'why are you in a wheelchair' is it when a shop assistant insists you can't possibly be able to push a trolley around a store or carry your shopping so insists on doing it for you, is it when someone decides that you would be better at a table your chair won't fit under so you can see the nice view, rather than a table the chair fits under so you can eat easily, is it when someone starts messing with your hair when in a queue, or who decides that you can't fit down a foot path you have used for decades, and so your forced onto three main roads, to go to the same place as they know best.. is it when a total stranger starts to tell you how to park the van you have been driving for years, is it when people in the hospital don't know how to use a hoist so when they do it wrong won't accept guidance putting me at risk... so often people think they know what's best for me.... so often they are wrong....

Ableist intrusions demonstrate that mobility aids become a focal point for strangers to enact their perceptions about the capacity of disabled women. These have a paternalistic tone which includes the non-disabled public having superior knowledge about access needs. Mo, a trans man who at the time describes not 'passing' due to being early in his transition and was using his wheelchair at Disney World:

> Suddenly I feel someone pushing my chair for me. I turned around and this white woman had her hands on my chair, and was trying to "help" me. Honestly, I don't remember if she was trying to push me out of the way or actually get me where I wanted to go. I was at a loss for words and had no idea what to say—I knew this was a thing that happens to disabled people all too often, but I was hoping it wouldn't happen to me at the park. It felt violating, especially since I was away from my partner who usually helped me with my chair and would have stopped the woman if they had seen her. The worst part about it was the fact that it was in a public place, where other abled people saw this happen and probably even thought it noble. After that, I felt much more hesitant to use/sit in my chair without appearing to "actively" wheel it while away from my partner (e.g. if they were in line somewhere, ordering food, etc).

Again we see the sudden and unexpected nature of intrusion, coming from behind. There is a further understanding of the intimacy tied up with who has the right to touch the chair. In this case, Mo referred to his partner as the one who would usually help with the chair and this felt like a particularly unpleasant violation over who could offer care.

The wheelchair is not just a mobility aid, it can be an extension of the bodily self and bound up in corporeal experiences of being disabled in public (Papadimitriou, 2008). Bal, who describes herself as a part time wheelchair user, provided an example of a time when a man was leaning on the arm of her chair while on a train. She tells how he was 'basically leaning on my arm' and explained why:

> I strongly feel that my wheelchair is an extension of me. I wouldn't touch, pull or lean on a stranger and I certainly wouldn't drag them where I thought they needed to be. Wheeling myself is part of my independence and every time someone pushes me without my consent they take that away from me. I know that to other people the touching is innocent and they're trying to be helpful but they're needs to be greater awareness of how disabled people see their mobility aids and why pushing people without consent is wrong.

In being touched without her consent, Bal not only feels a sense of personal violation but also that her independence is being removed. These behaviours demonstrate aspects of Carol Thomas' distinction between barriers to doing and barriers to being (2007). Bal experiences someone not only stopping her from what she is trying to do, but also what she is trying to be.

As with wheelchair users, participants who were visually impaired experience similar intrusions depending upon which mobility aid they were using. For guide dog user Teagan, the challenging interruptions of strangers wanting to touch her dog made basic tasks 'untenable'. She noted that despite having a sign on her back saying 'do not touch me', 'people relentlessly come up and touch the dog which means she becomes disturbed'. Participant Siobhan described how people almost found it 'mandatory to interrupt or distract' her guide dog and that this then required her to do extra tasks to refocus. She described the constant intrusions and 'ableist verbal violence' which are detailed in this excerpt:

> Many of my experiences happen while grocery shopping, from drive-by petting to being forced to engage with someone asking intrusive questions, but they can also happen in any public setting. "Please don't pet him; he's working" has become my default greeting when interacting with strangers. People also don't understand he's still working when I have to sit down and rest because I don't feel well.

> Every single time we go anywhere in public, someone wants to pet him. I understand, he's cute, and absolutely adorable in his enthusiasm to be helpful. He's also working. It would be appalling to interrupt a paramedic helping someone, yet when the paramedic or personal aide has 4 legs and fur, it somehow becomes not only acceptable, but nearly mandatory to interrupt or distract him and ignore my objections. Once, a woman scolded him for breaking a heel to push me into a seat in order to keep me from falling. A man started petting him behind my back while I was looking for the cookies. A woman yelled from outside his alert zone "HI PRETTY PUPPY! I KNOW IM NOT SUPPOSED TO PET YOU..." I was so startled my dog had to do extra tasks to help me refocus on what I was supposed to be doing at that moment, and then only a few moments later, another woman started petting him without asking and didn't stop when I told her.

I have PTSD. Reaching to pet my dog is reaching into my personal space bubble, and his presence is a passive non-verbal signal to give me extra space. Stop. Do not touch without my express permission. I don't understand why that's such a difficult concept for so many.

Siobhan's contribution eloquently highlights many nuances of her experience as a guide dog user. Her story demonstrates the way that disabled women might verbalise their boundaries, but strangers will still prioritise their own needs and ignore them. This might include petting a guide dog when they have been clearly told not to. Importantly, the intrusive behaviour penetrates their 'personal space bubble' and privacy. In Siobhan's example, the exchange represents a disruption to the flow of her day.

Participants who were white cane users described their mobility aid not necessarily as a focal point of intrusive behaviours but as a signifier of disability that drew unwanted attention. Hannah described how she had only been a white cane user for a couple of weeks at that point and already had a story of someone grabbing her elbow while she was preparing to cross the road. She found this frustrating as she had been trained in using the cane and this undermined her confidence and skill. Similarly, Lisa talked of how when the cane makes contact with an object, people feel the need to intervene. Citing an incident at a Metro station in Washington DC she recalls a man grabbing both of her shoulders and that she had to explain that the 'cane was a tool to detect obstacles'. Denisha describes how forced assistance can ensue when some people spot her white cane:

Recently there were building works happening on a street near my house. One of the builders warned me that there was a cable on the pavement and I thanked him for the warning and told him that I could see it and would be careful. He didn't listen to a word I said but just grabbed my arm. I felt really upset, and asked him to let go, which he did, in some shock. I often feel that I am infantilised as a disabled woman, that there is a perception that I am unable to judge situations for myself, that my body is somehow public property, and that I should just be grateful for having complete strangers paw at me. I'm frustrated at how often my words go unheard – I feel robbed of my agency and independence. I really don't mind people asking or offering help, or verbally alerting me to situations, but I need them to listen when I say I'm fine.

These experiences speak to common misconceptions and stereotypes of disabled people as incompetent, a cause of immense frustration for both Guide dog users and those with white canes because these both require training and high levels of skill. This presents a conflict between how they feel about the skill required in using their mobility aid and the swiftness with which this denotes inability and incompetence. In Worth's (2013) study of how visually impaired young people develop strategies for moving in the city, she details how their youth and disability intersect so that they are perceived as being doubly dependent. Despite training in using mobility aids and a feeling of achievement in this accomplishment, the sighted majority 'have the power to deny visually impaired young people's attempts at becoming a competent spatial actor' (p.583). In the present study, gender and disability can also be seen to intersect in the perception that women need assistance in using technology as they lack competence and capacity.

Intrusive Questions

> The ableist point of view is also driven by curiosity, perceived as a 'right' to intrude, inquire, appropriate impairment as a public spectacle…'curiosity' may manifest itself in direct personal questions, unthinkable in 'normal discourse.' (Loja et al., 2012, p. 194)

As already noted above, ableist intrusions incorporate both physical and verbal encounters. Chief amongst the latter are what can be termed diagnostic exchanges, whereby strangers seek personal information about an individual's impairment (Calder-Dawe et al., 2020). Within this study, these typically fell into two categories—diagnostic doubts and diagnostic insults. For instance, Teagan spoke about people frequently doubting and questioning her visual impairment:

> People come up to me and wave their hands in front of my face and go well you don't look blind! If I travel on public transport people relentlessly call out questions when I should be allowed to remain quiet in my private space.

Sai noted similar comments and recalled an interaction with a drunk man:

He was ranting e.g. "we have you on camera", "we know you're not really blind", "stop faking it", etc. I ignored him, talking w\partner, but going full alert. He continued & got nearer, 2 cane lengths away. I told him calmly to kindly fuck off. He got more aggressive. "Make me", he said. So I yelled at the top of my lungs, "hey station staff, this guy is harassing me, please make him go away". He laughed.

Such remarks speak to disabled people being seen as secretive or deceptive. In Sai's encounter it shows how a response to hostility can quickly escalate, exposing disabled women to increasing threats of violence.

Diagnostic insults also often came after seemingly banal questions. Denise described the continual questioning which seems neutral but is actually framed as an assumed incompetence:

I am often asked intrusive and personal questions, without any introduction or asking if I mind. These are often about my dog, but also very personal questions such as my age, whether I live alone, my level of vision and what I can see.

I am often asked out of the blue by complete strangers where I am going. I refuse to answer this question because as a visually impaired woman I feel that this makes me vulnerable to being followed. It's a weird question – why does a stranger need to know? Asking me where I am going is not an offer of help. An assumption that I am incapable – are you lost? As assumption that I have other mobility issues – can you walk?

Disabled women's experiences of insulting questions situate them as objects of curiosity. Strangers seek an opportunity to learn but without the usual social etiquette that precedes personal questions. Gaia noted the patronising 'aren't you coping well' comments or the more direct 'what's wrong with you?'

Aside from diagnostic questions, participants in the project also talked about personal questions involving sexualised language. These exchanges are demonstrative of the way that gender and disability intertwine with women's experiences of being reduced to their attractiveness and how their body language was being 'read'. Ash, a wheelchair user, described being at an airport where a fellow passenger asked what was wrong with her and that she was too young and pretty to be in a wheelchair. This then followed with intrusive questions about her condition. Not only did Ash experience diagnostic doubts, but a message was conveyed to her that attractive people could not be disabled. Elle, who is a deaf woman, has had similar intrusions when on public transport:

> The harassment I've experienced ranges from a man more than twice my age shoving hand-written notes in my face on the tube (saying things like 'you're so gorgeous for a deaf girl' and 'will you go for a drink with me?'), to the numerous people who insist on speaking for me, thus taking my voice away.

Elle's story was typical of the way that comments affect the embodied sense of self, where there is a 'privileging of men's evaluation of their internal world over their own experience' (Vera-Gray, 2017, p. 83). For disabled women, it is the ableist privilege of both men and women that is damaging their sense of their own identity.

Perhaps unsurprisingly, comments about attractiveness were also used as insults to intrude into the lives of disabled women. Lisa, a wheelchair user described a not untypical interaction with a man:

> I was waiting alone at the bus stop, and a man came up to me, started chatting, then put his hand on my shoulder and knelt down right beside me, trying to make conversation even when I refused to engage with him. I told him something to the effect that his intentions could have been to rape me. He screamed back, "who would want to rape you!"

This sexualised commentary demonstrates the way that disabled women have their bodies judged according to ableist and gendered norms. Strangers drew on common stereotypes of disability in order to remind disabled participants of 'their place'. As we shall see in the next section, such insults were often a gateway to the enactment of sexual assault.

Sexual Assault

A ramp agent at my home airport refused to acknowledge that I had declined his assistance, saying no each time I asked him to stop pushing me. He pushed me so quickly that he hit the edge of the ramp and dumped me out of my chair. He groped both of my breasts and then walked away. When I complained to the airline they said he knew I was struggling and was only trying to help.

Genevieve's description of her sexual assault was one of many similar encounters described by participants in the study. Their stories revealed a pattern of men using the guise of being helpful in order to mask a sexual assault. Other instances shared by participants included being groped while a door was being held open or as an excuse for helping them to avoid danger. These often opportunistic intrusions would then transcend into abusive comments drawing on ableist stereotypes of disabled women as being unattractive or confused about what was happening. In this instance Genevieve reported the assault, but the perpetrators' dismissal of events was immediately believed—thereby leaning into a disablist belief of the undesirability of disabled women's bodies.

Events such as these remind disabled women that their bodies are subject to the male gaze, while simultaneously communicating a message that they are innately unattractive. Victimological literature is now replete with evidence of how victims of sexual assault are often blamed or not believed (Horvath & Brown, 2022). Less evident is how in the cases of disabled women, victim blaming has a particularly chilling effect. Not only are the perpetrators typically believed, but they are positioned as good citizens whose helpful actions have been unfairly spurned. Cerise demonstrates the marginalising effect of this interaction:

In my power chair I have been followed and stalked by men catcalling me saying stuff like you're too pretty to be in a wheelchair offering to give me an unwanted sympathy **** within public the unwanted touching tends to be less than when on crutches or manual wheelchairs. When I reported the stalking or street harassment people don't believe you or witnesses think it's hilarious and I should be flattered because society views us disabled people as non sexual non desirable completely erasing the power dynamics at play.

The continuum of sexual intrusion that some disabled women experience is often accompanied by ableist slurs which are framed around the undesirability of the disabled body. To report is to potentially face further mocking or humiliation, which reduces disabled women's experiences of sexual violence to something humorous. Zitzelsberger (2005) writes about the way that the experiences of disabled women are delimited and distanced from normative standards of 'acceptable bodies' (p. 399). In terms of sexual intrusions, this study found that disabled women's bodies were additionally invalidated as objects of desire.

Other sexual intrusions were based around men needing to demonstrate their own attractiveness or testing what they could get away with. Ven talked of an evening where she had faced two instances of sexual intrusion:

A man stopped me and made me feel his hair because he was proud of it and I couldn't see it. So he grabbed my hand and put it on his head. Then he took my hand and tried to show me his sex toys he had with him. I escaped just in time with the help of a nearby friend. Later while walking up the stairs out of the shops a group of men cornered me and groped me hoping that I couldn't report them or describe them.

The implication in Ven's experience is that perpetrators draw on assumptions about her ability to report and her believability as a victim. This often extended to people verbalising how they might use the impairment of disabled women in order to commit an assault. For example, Denise recounted an instance of a man grabbing her breasts and saying 'it's okay, she's blind, she can't do anything'. In this case she had a witness and they reported it to the police but there was no further action taken. Denise had provided many different examples of intrusive behaviours that she experienced on a daily basis which included being touched, grabbed and often being left bruised or injured. She described contact as 'startling, frightening and disorienting'.

The stories provided by participants revealed a commonality amongst disabled women of ableist intrusions that regularly manifested as invasive questioning, forced control over mobility aids, physical force, verbal abuse and even sexual violence. Collectively these form a continuum of violence that illustrates the precarity with which disabled women must navigate public spaces. Ableist intrusions reflect also the way that disabled women's bodies are reduced to 'things' which should be moved out of the way and controlled. The idea that they are autonomous individuals with wants and needs is ignored, even when they articulate it verbally. Intrusions also reveal the simultaneous perception of the disabled body as both useable and useless. The nature and ubiquity of ableist intrusions carry with them a significant emotional labour which will be examined in the next chapter.

REFERENCES

Butler, R., & Bowlby, S. (1997). Bodies and spaces: An exploration of disabled people's experiences of public space. *Environment and Planning D: Society and Space, 15*(4), 411–433. https://doi.org/10.1068/d150411

Calder-Dawe, O., Witten, K., & Carroll, P. (2019). Being the body in question: Young people's accounts of everyday ableism, visibility and disability. *Disability & Society, 35*, 132–155.

Gardner, C. (1995). *Passing by: Gender and public harassment.* University of California Press.

Horvath, M. A. H., & Brown, J. M. (Eds.). (2022). *Rape: Challenging contemporary thinking—10 years on* (2nd ed.). Routledge. https://doi.org/10.4324/9781003163800

Laniya, O. O. (2005). Street smut: Gender, media, and the legal power dynamics of street harassment, or hey sexy and other verbal ejaculations. *Columbia Journal of Gender and Law, 14*(1). https://doi.org/10.7916/cjgl.v14i1.2503

Loja, E., Costa, M. E., Hughes, B., & Menezes, I. (2012). Disability, embodiment and ableism: Stories of resistance. *Disability & Society, 28*(2), 190–203. https://doi.org/10.1080/09687599.2012.705057

Papadimitriou, C. (2008). Becoming en-wheeled: The situated accomplishment of re-embodiment as a wheelchair user after spinal cord injury. *Disability & Society, 23*(7), 691–704. https://doi.org/10.1080/09687590802469420

Thomas, C. (2007). *Sociologies of disability and illness. Contested ideas in disability studies and medical sociology.* Palgrave Macmillan.

Vera-Gray, F. (2017). *Men's intrusion, women's embodiment: A critical analysis of street harassment.* Routledge.

Worth, N. (2013). Visual impairment in the city: Young people's social strategies for independent mobility. *Urban Studies, 50*(3), 574–586. https://doi.org/10.1177/0042098012468898

Zitzelsberger, H. (2005). (In)visibility: Accounts of embodiment of women with physical disabilities and differences. *Disability & Society, 20*(4), 389–403. https://doi.org/10.1080/09687590500086492

CHAPTER 5

The Ableist Atmosphere

Abstract The chapter provides a deeper examination of the ableist nature of public space. This focuses on who is doing the intruding and what their potential motivation says about how disabled women are viewed. What is revealed is the benevolent ableism which draws on stereotypes of disabled people as weak and in need of assistance. For participants who experienced sexual abuse from men, the motivation was similarly dismissed based on the notion that disabled women were not sexual beings and must have misunderstood what was happening. These important findings are examined in relation to the intersection of gender and disability and how some bodies are seen as undesirable, damaged and/or weak. The chapter details new insights into how perpetrators of intrusions are both men and women. The chapter also provides an examination of the emotional labour required of disabled women by looking at their reactions to ableist intrusions. It will show how they balance concerns about safety and risk while also wanting to demonstrate their frustration at the ubiquity of intrusions. The chapter will discuss the way that atmospheres are felt and sensed, leading to a reflection on the role of instinct in assessing unwanted intrusions.

Keywords Emotional labour · Safety work · Ableist anxiety · Benevolent ableism

H. Mason-Bish, *Disability, Gender, Bodies and Boundaries*, Palgrave Hate Studies, https://doi.org/10.1007/978-3-031-85890-1_5

63

I Was Only Trying to Help

The previous chapter outlined a typology of the intrusive behaviours that disabled women experience when moving about in public space. A broad pattern of ableism was established and framed in the context of the everyday actions which form part of the contours of daily life. The overwhelming discourse that was used to explain ableist intrusions was around the intentions of the public who claimed they were being helpful. Strangers would touch first, and then verbalise that they were 'trying to help'. Gabby, who described herself as having mild cerebral palsy and hydrocephalus detailed one example:

> A lady saw me hobbling around (my leg particularly hurt that day) and came from behind to ask me for help by grabbing my arm and talking in a raised voice. Her grabbing me caused my arm to spasm, which really hurts and I can then feel uncomfortable for ages after. The lady was actually very kind and helpful but I don't believe that grabbing/touching someone makes you more helpful, especially as you have no idea how that person would feel.

What Gabby's story demonstrates is that while the intentions of strangers might be kind, the result can be to cause pain and discomfort. Instead, participants in the research often expressed the way that help should involve consent and a verbalised question about what might be an appropriate and useful interaction. Shona, a guide dog user, described a similar encounter to Gabby, which began helpfully but shifted when her words were ignored. Writing in the third person, she explained:

> Shona was walking along a familiar street with her guide dog, when the dog suddenly slowed, Making her aware of a pavement obstacle. Shona could hear work going on ahead so stood for a minute until a man approached her.. he explained that there was a ladder on the pavement but that he would give her assistance to get past it. He then told Shona to take his hand to which she explained that she would hold his elbow so that he could guide her safely. As she took his elbow he grabbed her elbow and in doing so touched her rib cage. However accidental this may have been, Shona felt powerless in the situation and felt that her explanation of how best to help had been ignored. She also felt that she had been touched in an inappropriate and intimate place, which would have been easily avoided had the person listened to her original advice. He then proceeded to walk past the ladder not explaining that there was not enough space for the three

of them including the dog. This led to both Shona and the dog becoming confused and disorientated as they were not able to use the skills of their partnership in the correct way as they would have normally done when using sighted guide. Shona wishes that people would #justaskdon'tgrab, but also wants to stress the importance of listening when a disabled person tells you how best to be helpful and respond appropriately.

Conversely, Tai, who is a wheelchair user described how people would often suddenly start pushing them without any words at all. Such encounters were 'terrifying' and exacerbated by the fact that 'they refuse to believe you when you insist you don't want help'. Sometimes these encounters become increasingly aggressive. April described an incident where the forceful help was persistent and angry:

> I suddenly had a woman (i would say in her late forties), shouting at me that there was a car coming. I replied in a friendly way telling her that I knew. A couple of minutes later, the next car drove past us and she did the same, now walking next to my guide dog. I responded in a harsher voice telling her that I knew and that she should have realised that as I had just told my son to watch out for the car. I asked my son to ride his bike faster and got my guide dog to walk faster in an attempt to get away from the woman as she almost walked into my guide dog. Then the third car came and she grabbed my left arm, reaching over my guide dog, and tried to pull me around. She was actually trying to pull me into the road as my dog always walks on the side facing the road. I tried to pull my arm away but she held on and shouted to me about the car and that I needed to know that. Once I managed to pull my arm away, I walked really fast and we finally got rid of her as she couldn't keep up.

April's example demonstrates the way that disabled women's voices are ignored by strangers who assume that they lack capacity to make decisions about their own safety. Even when making a deliberate effort to be assertive, and ratcheting up the tone of that request, they might find themselves ignored. This infantilisation of disabled people is a common experience in many aspects of their lives where other people assume they can make decisions for them (Beckwith & Drake, 2022; Hughes, 2009). Participants in the study also commented that strangers intruding on them would not listen when other people spoke up. For example, Petra uses a cane occasionally and described a case of a man forcefully grabbing her:

This man could not take no for an answer, even when my partner turned to me and asked and I said. The man continued to pester my partner to convince me to move "because it would be better". This man I did not know was convinced he knew what was best for me, better than myself and my partner. As someone with EDS, grabbing and shaking me is one of the worst things you can do. He did not understand why he couldn't just touch me. I felt awful and like I wasn't being listened to.

The forceful nature of help is an aspect of benevolent ableism. It is a kind of microaggression which reinforces the notion that disabled people are lesser and lacking in capacity. The *ability* of the person 'helping' is enacted in these encounters as a physical demonstration of what a 'normal' body can do. The assumption of required help can be understood through the legacy of 'charitable inclinations' towards disabled people which turns them into 'objects of benefaction' (Loja et al., 2012, p. 193). The non-disabled public conceive of the disabled body as an object without agency, consent or knowledge. At best participants described being treated like children. AJ who has a form of proportional dwarfism, talked of this:

The list goes on, but the main issue is that people assume I need help (I understand they want to and don't mind them asking first) or treat me like a child, despite the fact that I am a woman, and they actually end up invading my personal space.

The paternalistic tone of these intrusions means that strangers overstep the mark in that a 'helpful' intention becomes personal invasive. To add to this, it can be particularly galling for disabled women who might be highly trained in using their mobility aid. Hannah, who describes herself as visually impaired and moderately deaf, talked of how even though she had only been using a cane for two weeks, she already had a story:

I had been out and was on my way home, so headed to the crossing, went to put my hand where the spinner is, when someone to my left said something to me. I didn't hear as I'm also moderately to severely deaf in both ears. Then as the spinner went, I put my cane back in the right hand and felt her touch my arm as I went to walk. As I was moving forward and she hadn't (I presume), it felt like a pull. It really angered me as I'm obviously trained so am fully aware how to cross the road safely. I was never even asked if I wanted help!

The mobility aid is a visual signifier of disability, but the public may perceive it as indicative of incompetence warranting help, rather than something which might suggest a level of skill. Sam who is non-binary and autistic talked about how people would mistake their 'wariness for help-lessness' meaning that people are reading their physical appearance and behaviour and making their own interpretation. This is even more the case because of the location where the enforced help or intrusion occurs. In Lenney and Sercombe's (2002) work on encounters with disabled people in public places, they talk of symbols and situations that can frame the interaction. In titling their article 'Did you see that guy in the wheelchair down the pub?' they speak of the shock and surprise that people express when seeing a disabled person out in public. In the context of a pub, a convivial and social space, they are less likely to expect to see a disabled person having fun. This then leads to the reaction described by Jax:

> From people trying to help me onto a train and dropping the wheelchair onto its back, drunken people trying to help me into a pub and endangering my life by mistake, I have found that People are frightened by wheelchairs and rarely ask the person or even see them. I believe that most people mean well however there are some people out there that have taken advantage.

Other participants talked about intrusions at music festivals or social events where people were publicly, loudly, expressing their intention to help. This performative aspect of help, where the desire to be seen to be helpful overrides further the desires and needs of the disabled person is an important part of understanding these (un)helpful interactions. Siobhan, a service dog user, sums up the way that 'help' is used to frame the ableist intrusions that she experiences:

> My first reaction is to knock you into next week for your ableist verbal violence in self defence....'I was just trying to be friendly!' No you weren't. You invaded my boundaries, likely caused me physical pain, definitely caused me distress, and I neither want nor need your ableist pity.

The 'just trying to be friendly' comment acts as a form of plausible denia-bility designed to frame the disabled person as an ungrateful recipient. But it is also based on a desire to help due to pity. In Papadimitriou's (2008) work, the intrusion might be framed around friendliness or benevolence, but is because disabled people are not regarded as 'active doers'. Instead, they are a 'dilemma of negotiation, reorganizing and reconfiguring social relations' (Papadimitriou, 2008). Women generally experience these kinds of unhelpful intrusions, commonly described as 'mansplaining' or patronising assumptions of help. Disabled women are therefore more likely to be viewed as helpless, which makes intrusions more likely. People intrude because they feel they need to, because they are anxious when seeing a disabled woman who is 'out of place' (Kitchin, 1998).

Disabled participants also spoke of the way that atmospheres would shift and that the silence of bystanders served to reinforce the actions of the person touching them. Aisha spoke about this in the context of an interaction between her, another disabled person and a member of the public. In this situation diagnostic assessments were happening, with the stranger determining who was the most disabled and how to respond:

I was walking at my normal slow pace with my walking stick along the pavement and a mobility scooter user (nice person) was coming the other way. I had more than enough space to change direction and move out of the nice person's way, and started to do so, but then a nasty person who was in the process of overtaking me thrust their arm out and pushed me off the pavement into the road to make way for the nice person. The nice person apologised but the nasty person seemed to think they had done the right thing, and kept their arm there until the nice person had passed. Then the nasty person walked away, not looking back at me. I had no energy to respond to any of this and just had to stand there and then slowly make my way back on to the pavement. I was lucky that I only ended up in the bike lane and there were no bikes coming. I felt anger and confusion and embarrassment. There is no such thing as a disability hierarchy and yet here is another able-bodied person feeling good about themselves for deciding which one of us was less capable at that point. I thought that maybe the nasty person didn't see my stick, and thought I was being rude, and then felt defensive about their decision and decided to stick with it not apologise, but why should I be rationalising their movements? The nice person was more than capable of asking one or both of us to kindly make room for them, and they didn't because they could see that I was in the process of turning. The nasty person could have come to the conclusion that there might be a reason why I'm walking so slowly (or could have clocked the darn walking stick), and recognised that I needed more time to move out of the way. This is a concurrent experience in my life – I need to stop letting people off for these things as that usually means that the blame shifts onto myself. In my wider experience, the ability to walk seems to be a sign of a higher position in the fake disability hierarchy. But what if

I find walking difficult? What if I'm in a lot of pain? What if I simply can't afford a wheelchair? What if I have a changeable position and I'm okay right now but know that I'm going to crash in a minute? Another thing that comes into this is age – I am below 25 years old and this also seems to signal HEALTH to anyone and everyone who doesn't understand that young people can be sick too. I'm sick (pun intended) of people assuming that they know more about my condition than I do. I'm tired (pun also intended – I have M.E.) of not being allowed the space to move through the world at my own pace, in whatever way is easiest for me. As long as I am not hurting anybody else, I would like a society that refrains from hurting me.

The constant judgements about the nature of impairment can have an exhausting effect. The emotional labour of ableist intrusions will be explored later on but suffice to say that for many participants a frustrating part of (un)helpful intrusions was the way that people thought they were 'being noble' (Mo) or as 'a prop to show how "good" they are either to themselves or others' (Cerise). Hughes (2012) writes about the way that people 'convert pity to social capital' in their interactions with disabled people because it 'confirms their status as a benevolent person'. To be told that help is not required is a crushing blow to their sense of self and their performative benevolence. Participants pointed out that it was not that they didn't appreciate help, but that their consent should be sought and that it should not be performative and loud. Help should be respectful and quiet.

THE KNIGHT IN SHINING ARMOUR

The gendered aspect of (un)helpful intrusions is demonstrated by the reality that women are more likely to be perceived as lacking capacity and not knowing what they need (Garland-Thomson, 2001). However, it is also interesting to explore the gender of the people doing the intruding. Many participants referred to encounters with men and the power relations at play. Neira talked of the way that men often think they are acting as a type of saviour:

The most recent example is a common one – this time the person who attempted to "help" was someone who had come to my house to do some work for me. Because his van was on my drive way, I was on the edge of the tarmac and my wheels fell into a muddy patch. It would have probably taken me twenty seconds to get out of the mud, but after five seconds this man was attempting to drag the chair, despite asking him not to and telling him that he could hurt himself (but thanks anyway). So now I was truly stuck with this man heaving and huffing and painfully rocking me about. Eventually, I had to perform the necessary maneuver only very very slowly so to avoid hurting him (although that was mostly luck). I'm sure he thought he had performed a rescue.

This physical demonstration of strength and prowess highlights the role of masculinity in overt displays of unwanted help. This chimes with literature on street harassment more generally where intrusive acts are about men performing masculinity and gaining power by putting women in their place (Hindes & Fileborn, 2023). The understanding that men might have intentions to sexually assault meant that participants might be particularly cautious in some situations. Ali described this:

Generally speaking, if I show distress or fall down, a man will try to help me... I'm fine with the offer of help, usually, but you should never touch someone without their consent. Being touched by strange men like this has led me to have nightmares and made me more uncomfortable around men in general.

If the disabled female body is read as being in need of help and showing any signs of distress, then an unwanted intrusion might happen. In the previous chapter I detailed the times that women had experienced sexual assault which means that the unwanted touching carries a level of threat and fear of escalation. However, this is compounded by their disability because it may make them feel particularly vulnerable. Elle explains this:

I've become a wheelchair user in the last year. I live in a small town in a rural area. Each time I have gone out on my own I have had men (always men over a certain age) stop and stare at me openly! I feel so vulnerable that I no longer venture out alone. I used to run long distance, but now I feel that if I was attacked, followed, or any unwanted attention, I wouldn't be able to get away or avoid it. It would be so easy for anyone to follow me home. I feel trapped.

Elle is drawing together the way that disabling moments are framed also by her gendered understanding of women's safety. Having previously been a runner she knew about the potentiality of men's violence but felt that her 'safety work' was possible. Now, she feels that she cannot put measures in place to mitigate against this risk. Her mobility aid marks her out as a disabled woman and so she feels trapped rather than freed when using it.

The responses of some men to being asked not to touch the participants demonstrate the way that hostility is embedded in the intention behind the touch. For example, Genevieve spoke of a time when she shouted at someone not to touch her and the man told her 'not to get hysterical'. Such gendered language was also demonstrated in encounters such as that of Cerise:

> In one case I was sitting in my chair on a pavement waiting for my friends car and a man literally just grabbed my chair and wheeled me across the road to 'help' despite my shouts for help and that I didn't even want to cross the road. I genuinely thought I was being kidnapped. He was completely baffled when I wouldn't stop shouting and telling him to get the hell off me and was really angry at me for not 'appreciating his help' and called me an ungrateful bitch and said fuck you cripple to me.

This example demonstrates the way that refusals of 'help' can be seen as a form of public shaming and what can follow is an angry and hostile reaction from the person intruding. The intersection of gender and disability is also evidenced by the response in this example of a man calling her a bitch and a cripple which is both gendered and ableist language. Sometimes this type of forced assistance is persistent. Elle described a situation where she was labelled ungrateful by a man in a restaurant:

> He insisted that he would place my order, telling me to put my phone away and sign what I wanted to him instead. Again, I told him "no". At this point, he began to get upset. "WHY?" he yelled and signed. "I am deaf every day – I think I know how to handle these things myself", I signed back. "I really don't need your help." The man continued to argue with me about why he, as a hearing person, was better placed to order my drink for me, despite my (now numerous) requests for him to stop and leave me alone. He also expressed frustration about how 'ungrateful' I was being. When the barman approached to take my order, the man proceeded to tell the barman that I was deaf and he would place my order on my behalf. Again, I said "NO", this time raising my voice. I then informed the barman that I was being harassed. The barman told the man to leave me alone, and he finally backed away. Now, as I reflect on the incident,

a whole host of questions come to mind. What part of 'no' did the man not understand in the first place? Why did he continue to disrespect my boundaries and ignore my requests to be left alone? Why did he only back down when a warning came from another (hearing) male? As a (Deaf) woman, am I not allowed to have the same boundaries as others?

Although participants talked a lot about men using their power to intimidate disabled women, many recounted stories where the person intruding was a woman. This was particularly the case in instances of forced help was almost a type of patronising 'mother knows best'. Emma described a situation where she was unloading shopping and a checkout operator stood up and grabbed the basket from her lap. In doing so she knocked the joystick of the wheelchair causing it to jolt forward. This silent encounter has a matriarchal air where Emma felt she was being treated like a naughty child. Danielle talked of an incident on a bus where a woman tried to grab her rucksack, again silently and misguidedly attempting to help. The difference with men's intrusions was the aggressive labelling of them as ungrateful or hysterical and the underlying threat of escalation or potential sexual assault. But the need to regulate disabled women's bodies affects how both able-bodied men and women behave.

Hostility, Escalation and Belittling Responses

Ableist intrusions are not neatly packaged encounters. They encompass sometimes complicated emotions and intentions that shift. In sharing their stories, participants were aware of this and described how they would sense a change of atmosphere or tone of voice which was telling about the intentions of the people touching them. Alyssa spoke of an encounter in an elevator which was crowded and a man grabbed her by the shoulders to manoeuvre her into position. She told him firmly not to touch her and he told her to 'calm down'. As she reached for the buttons on the elevator wall he grabbed her again:

> I yelled, "What did I just tell you?" A man near the back of the elevator joked, "You can touch me if you want." Everyone laughed. As I got off the elevator, a couple of people yelled comments about how I was getting upset over nothing. I'll never forget how angry and hopeless I felt, having

an elevator full of people side with a man who touched me without consent and laugh at me for trying to defend myself, and not being able to do a thing about it.

This hostile and unsupportive reaction by others in the lift served to not only undermine Alyssa's anger at being touched but at how it made her feel powerless. It is indicative about the power relations at play when bodies connect in this way. If it can be perceived as a form of 'help', then the reaction of dismissive anger and humiliation do not suggest a genuine benevolence. The help is performative, non-consensual and forced. This is a familiar and routine part of being a woman in public, where the only accepted response to catcalling is to laugh or ignore it. An integral part of safety work is to deflect what might 'really' be happening by smiling along or having no response at all (Vera-Gray, 2018, p. 154). For disabled women, the expected reaction is acquiescence. Yasmin talked about the way that even encounters which do not escalate to anger instead feature people seeming put out by the refusal of 'help'.

> I have had some people be apologetic when I respond to them but they tend to then follow it quickly with a justification, "oh I was only trying to help" or "you looked like you were struggling" or they will just shrug and look bemused as if I am being so ungrateful.

Mina spoke of how she is always polite when she declines help and might try and use it as an educative moment. But this results in people ignoring her:

> People feel so entitled to just touch me and push me and cross those boundaries. And when I tell people to stop and explain how my fingers can get caught, the reaction has been just as strange. Sometimes people look at me like I'm ungrateful, and at other times they completely shut down and ignore me and what I'm trying to tell them, as if I'm not worth speaking or listening to. I've literally had people turn their backs on me once I start talking to them and explaining that they should just ask first! It's really that simple! And it's not like I'm screaming at them, I start with a "Thanks, but next time...." but it's no use.

Earlier I detailed the way that unwanted touching might happen in silence, without even an attempt to ask or offer assistance. The angry reaction to rejection might be the first time that the stranger speaks to the disabled woman. Lisa is a wheelchair user and gives two examples of this immediate hostility and quick shift in atmosphere.

> I was waiting to cross a street in Queens, New York with my guide dog when a guy came up from behind my right side and started pushing me by my right arm. I stood still and raised the arm so he would lose his grip and pass by. He said nothing until he was mad I didn't accept him pushing me out into the street.

> People have tried to grab my metro card (which we use to pay for the NYC subway) when they saw my guide dog and that my first swipe didn't work. They are always angry when I don't let them have it, even though I don't know them and they don't speak first.

These situational aspects of ableist intrusions demonstrate a dynamic aspect of unwanted touching where strangers are trying to remove the friction that they observe in a disabled person taking time to cross a road or pay for a train ticket. The busy city environment is an ableist place, where forced help is about moving the disabled person on rather than actively assisting.

Emotional Labour and Assessing the Atmosphere

Disabled women in this research talked about their own reactions to unwanted touching and intrusions. These included emotional reactions and verbal ones. Most commonly, they spoke of having no response at all or a muted, polite one. This comes from weighing up potential danger and escalation even in the most benign of encounters. Anya who uses a powerchair, spoke of a time when someone grabbed her arm and said 'god bless you' as if she were some sort of healer. Just wanting to escape the situation, Anya said thank you:

> I was furious and frustrated. I wanted to tell her to "fuck off!" but since becoming disabled, I can't run away from a fight so have to be polite, but then after I am angry at them, but also at my body as I can't defend myself as I could when I was able bodied.

In sharing their stories, participants often described the deep embodiment of each intrusive encounter. The reaction that they give might not be their real self, but a protective mechanism to avoid escalation. In Anya's example, it is possible to see the way that disabled women might reflect on their disability and feel frustrated by it. This can bring them to an 'unwanted consciousness of [their] impaired body' (Paterson & Hughes, 1999, p. 603). She is also making what Fiona Vera-Gray describes as the escalation calculation (Vera-Gray, 2018). Women evaluate situations based on the people present, whether they might be accused of causing or provoking violence against them and if it might escalate. This emotional labour is evident in Anya's description. Ali is a non-binary person with invisible disabilities including dyspraxia and describes an incident when they were 15 and had fallen over. A man offered help but even a 'no thank you' was ignored as he grabbed under Ali's arms:

> it was SO UNCOMFORTABLE. The physical contact hurt because I was already overwhelmed with sensory input from the fall and the heat, and I just did not want a man so much bigger and stronger than me touching me anyway. I pushed him off of me as gently as I could and walked inside, but I felt violated.

In this situation Ali observes the strength of the man, meaning that even though it was painful, they still felt that they had to respond in a quiet and gentle manner to diffuse further escalation. A related phenomena is the way that participants described a ratcheting of their response when they are in a dangerous situation. Denise detailed how she would begin with a polite request for someone to let go, but if their grip becomes too tight and she thinks they are trying to drag her then her 'request is usually louder or more insistent. However, in the split second that the grab occurs, it's not always possible to discern the difference'. The emotional labour and exhaustion that this causes is significant because it is such a precarious and changeable situation which can escalate quickly. Goodley et al. (2017) describe this as a particularly skilled form of inter-personal labour required to navigate these situations. Importantly, it extends beyond these types of stranger intrusions and into interactions with carers, educators, health care professionals and beyond.

In reading situations and thinking about how to respond, participants spoke about sensory interpretations of the atmosphere they found themselves in. Sometimes their response would be to disrupt the space, loudly, by making a clear noise. Mina described 'yelling' in a man's face after he pushed her chair after a period of touching her, to which he merely mumbled and left her alone. Others spoke of shouting or screaming; making an unusual disruptive noise so as to shift the atmosphere of what might otherwise be a silent encounter. This juxtaposition of noise and peace was commonly talked about in terms of assessing safe spaces. For example, Kerry described the way that 'navigating the city as a disabled woman comes with a drain of energy' which encompassed issues of access and mobility as well as unwanted interactions with the public. Such spaces have a volatility where a wheelchair user is encountering the physical ableist design which then requires focus and skill to get around. Intrusions have a penetrative effect which may punctuate this quiet focus. Fontaine (2021) describes street harassment as creating 'affective atmospheres of unwelcome' which connect women to the bodily self. In this instance, unwanted touch is interrupting a quietness and privacy. Teagan articulates this; 'I should be allowed to remain quiet in my private space' because intrusions force a reaction of some sort and emotion work in managing feelings. This means that they must 'alternate between the self and the other, adjusting actions and responses in relation to those projected by and for the other' (Vera-Gray, 2018, p. 77).

This chapter has provided an examination of the interaction between disabled women and strangers in the context of unwanted intrusions. Sometimes motivated by benevolent ableism, people might verbalise their reason for intruding which draws on stereotypes of disabled bodies as being in a permanent state of helplessness. A closer reading of the exchanges demonstrates the way they might swiftly become hostile encounters when offers of help are refused. Ableist intrusions are perpetrated by both men and women, demonstrating that disabled women's bodies are subject to a negative gaze and need to be regulated from a variety of viewpoints. The consequence of potential intrusion is to force disabled women to undertake significant emotional labour, be on their guard and use their senses to anticipate how a situation might develop. The impacts of this on their daily life and deeper sense of self will be examined in the next chapter.

References

Beckwith, D., & Drake, G. (2022). Exploring women's experiences of sexuality education, sexual expression and violence: Inclusive research with disabled women. *Disability & Society, 39*(2), 422–434. https://doi.org/10.1080/096 87599.2022.2071677

Fontaine, J. (2021). When girls walk: Mobilities of and resistance to affective atmospheres of unwelcome. *Space and Culture, 25*, 633–644.

Garland-Thomson, R. (2001). *Re-shaping, re-thinking, re-defining: Feminist disability studies* (The Barbara Waxman Fiduccia Papers on Women and Girls with Disabilities). Center for Women Policy Studies. https://bpb-us-e2.wpm ucdn.com/sites.middlebury.edu/dist/1/4371/files/2020/03/Garland-Tho mson_Redefining_Feminist_Disabilities_Studies_2001.pdf

Goodley, D., Liddiard, K., & Runswick-Cole, K. (2017). Feeling disability: Theories of affect and critical disability studies. *Disability & Society, 33*(2), 197–217. https://doi.org/10.1080/09687599.2017.1402752

Hindes, S., & Fileborn, B. (2023). "Why did he do it? Because he's a Fucking Bloke": Victim insights into the perpetration of street harassment. *British Journal of Criminology, 63*(3), 668–686. https://doi.org/10.1093/bjc/aza c029

Hughes, B. (2009). Wounded/monstrous/abject: A critique of the disabled body in the sociological imaginary. *Disability & Society, 24*, 399–410.

Hughes, B. (2012). Fear, pity and disgust: Emotions and the non-disabled imaginary. In N. Watson, A. Roulstone & C. Thomas (Eds.), *Routledge handbook of disability studies* (1st ed., pp. 67–78). Routledge.

Kitchin, R. (1998). "Out of place", "knowing one's place": Space, power and the exclusion of disabled people. *Disability & Society, 13*(3), 343–356. https:// doi.org/10.1080/09687599826678

Lenney, M., & Sercombe, H. (2002). 'Did you see that guy in the wheelchair down the pub?' Interactions across difference in a public place. *Disability & Society, 17*(1), 5–18. https://doi.org/10.1080/09687590120100093

Loja, E., Costa, M. E., Hughes, B., & Menezes, I. (2012). Disability, embodiment and ableism: Stories of resistance. *Disability and Society, 28*(2), 190–203. https://doi.org/10.1080/09687599.2012.705057

Papadimitriou, C. (2008). 'It was hard but you did it': The co-production of 'work' in a clinical setting among spinal cord injured adults and their physical therapists. *Disability & Rehabilitation, 30*(5), 365–374.

Paterson, K., & Hughes, B. (1999). Disability studies and phenomenology: The carnal politics of everyday life. *Disability & Society, 14*(5), 597–610.

Vera-Gray, F. (2018). *The right amount of panic: How women trade freedom for safety in public*. Policy Press.

CHAPTER 6

Living a Smaller Life: Impacts of Ableist Intrusions

Abstract In this chapter the impacts of ableist intrusions are detailed. The chapter shows disabled women limit their daily movements in order to avoid intrusive behaviours. This involves changing routes home even when these routes are less accessible or foregoing their mobility aid so as not to appear visibly disabled. This has significant impacts on their physical and emotional wellbeing. It is often in addition to injuries sustained during the unwanted intrusions where disabled women might be placed in danger or have serious harm caused to them. On a broader level, impacts can involve changing their personality so as to appear 'smaller' or avoiding social or work situations where possible. The impacts of these will be clearly articulated as they can result in disabled women being excluded from public life altogether. This will involve looking at not only the emotion work that they are carrying out in managing their lived experiences, but also how this creates a society which is not inclusive and equitable.

Keywords Harms · Embodiment · Psycho-emotional disablism · Ableism · Safety work

In Harms Way

Ableist intrusions can cause both physical and psychological harms which cause disabled women to limit and alter their daily movements in order to avoid being touched.

This is often in addition to injuries sustained during the unwanted intrusions where they might be placed in real physical danger. Being touched without consent caused some disabled women physical pain and harm. Pippa describes herself as someone with multiple allergies including to lanolin, pollen, and dust mites, to name but a few.

> As if this is not obnoxious enough, some people (I have noticed especially old women) seem to feel a need to seek out exposed skin and touch it. They go for my hands, even when I tell them not to they do it all the more. I blister, my skin bleeds, my hands are sore.

This demonstrates an ageist dynamic which other researchers have also uncovered. In interactions with older strangers, disabled people can face particular assumptions about their lack of capacity (Wayland et al., 2020; Worth, 2013). In Pippa's example, her verbal request for desistance was ignored by an older woman who felt that she knew better. Other participants found that beyond verbal requests, sometimes their physical demonstration of pain was not enough to stop people touching them. Lucy described how visible signs of pain are not enough to prevent the harmful results of being touched:

> I have fibromyalgia and chronic pain amongst other issues since 2008. One of my symptoms is allodynia – which means that my nervous system is faulty and will send a pain signal instead of a "touch" signal – so even the lightest touch can feel like I've been punched, hit with a sledgehammer, tazered or shot. The pain is like a lightning bolt and can make my muscles go into agonising spasms. If I'm standing it can drop me to the ground. constantly patting me EVEN when I've told them not to, such as saying "please don't touch, it HURTS", they'll then reach out to pat me AGAIN in response, either in apology or as if I'm being silly. I often wear a badge by stick man communications that says "don't touch me without asking. Thanks", but it doesn't always work. When people get too close I try to back away if possible, and if I can't move my powerchair away I will visibly flinch away from them if they look like they are about to try and touch me, but often they just reach further to pat me even when it's plainly obvious that I'm cringing away from it and raising my hands in defence.

Disabled women might provide clear directions to strangers including showing physical signs such as the raising of hands in pain, yet the touching persists. Other physical pains that participants described including the shock or anxiety of being touched causing an angina attack and disorientation (Jem), being left with bruising (Denise) and having their back twisted causing them to scream out in pain (Anje). Gabby talked of leg spasms due to being grabbed which really hurt and were 'uncomfortable for ages after'. As well as pain caused from the unwanted touching, participants also spoke of it being compounded by situations where they had hurt themselves or fallen. Ali, who has multiple disabilities which make falling over a frequent occurrence, described a situation where they fell and someone rushed over to ask if help was required. Ali described how they politely declined and when they fell again the stranger grabbed them. This exacerbated any initial pain:

> The physical contact hurt because I was already overwhelmed with sensory input from the fall and the heat.

Ali goes on to detail a second incident when they were fumbling for a key to open a door and someone rushed behind them and took control:

> I didn't actually notice him approach; he just said "let me do it" and took the key out of my hand. The touch BURNED badly and I reflexively backhanded him in the chest (because I was having a meltdown). I'm not sure how he reacted because my perception of the situation wasn't clear, but I ended up in my room on my bed with the key sitting on the dresser.

While in some encounters the ableist anxiety of the person intruding would not be to cause intentional harm, the assumption of disabled weakness and lack of agency or autonomy means that even pleas not to be touched are ignored. Charlie provided an interesting insight into this as someone more recently disabled with a neurological condition who reflected on their own encounters beforehand. She recalls an instance from years previously where a friend with ME had a personal tragic event:

> My instinct is to offer hugs and reassuring pats and back rubs when someone is in emotional pain. I completely forgot how his condition affects him and kept touching and hugging him. I meant well, but I didn't appreciate the physical pain I was inflicting upon him. It's difficult to understand how even the lightest touch can cause so much agony to some people. I

have since been diagnosed with my own neurological disease and, over the last decade, I have come to learn for myself just how painful the simplest touch can be. I'm only sorry that it took my own lived experience to fully comprehend what I inflicted upon my friend all those years ago. The old adage about walking a mile in another man's moccasins is very true indeed.

Charlie describes the lack of knowledge she had for disability and how impairments can cause pain which she only realised when becoming disabled herself. This speaks to the previous chapter, where motivations of strangers can be blurry and unclear.

Psychological Harms

The impacts of unwanted intrusive behaviours had both physical and psychological impacts. Alyssa provided the story of the time she was training her new guide dog and in attendance with a large group of other students, one of whom sexually assaulted her twice. She was not believed by the facilitators who she reported it to. She described what happened next:

> Once I got home, I fell into a deep depression over how I'd been treated. I began to have panic attacks and couldn't work.

She has since had therapy but the persistent touching by strangers triggers her fear and re- traumatises her and the sense of shame she had at the time. For disabled women who experience unwanted intrusions, a higher state of alert and internalised danger is created. Gaia provided an example of this and the way that previous experiences had caused her to be scared of being in the city alone and that 'even when it doesn't happen, I am scared of it happening'. A sense of safety is therefore an embodied experience whereby fear is felt because of the potential of what might happen. It is also spatially specific, as Gaia describes a particular context of being in the city and alone. As Edward and Maxwell (2021) state, feelings of (un)safety are both transient and situational but are importantly 'felt' in the body. This can be best demonstrated in the account of Lucy who described the negative associations caused by repeated encounters with strangers:

It makes me incredibly nervous about being out and about because physical contact in the wrong place (like my back or upper arms) is so painful, it has created an anxious negative association with crowds and strangers – if every time you were in that situation someone poked you with a cattle prod, you would no doubt develop the same anxiety over contact by repeated negative reinforcement.

Again, it is context specific in relation to crowds and strangers, but her nerves and anxiety are viscerally described by her analogy in this quote. A cattle prod is a painful but also particular tool to get animals to move where you want them to go. Disabled women experience the psychological harms of being repeatedly touched and the serious pain that it can cause them, leading to a state of fear or alert when in those situations. Being in crowds was another example of a fearful context because they are an uncontrollable environment without much space and where it is easier for people to intrude.

STRATEGIES AND SAFETY WORK

That women carry out safety work and develop strategies to avoid danger in public spaces is something uncontested in feminist literature. Developed by academic Liz Kelly, safety work can be understood as the repertoire of behaviours and tasks that women do on a regular, sometimes subconscious level to feel safe. Examples might include avoiding certain areas, changing/wearing particular clothes or not engaging with people who are perceived as a threat (Vera-Gray & Kelly, 2020). In this research, participants spoke of the sorts of things that they did to avoid being touched by strangers. In the previous section we heard from Pippa who spoke about the way that her allergies caused intense physical pain if touched. She finds herself having to wear a jacket even during hot weather which makes her then feel dehydrated and sick. But she describes it as necessary in order to protect herself from the extreme pain she suffers if she is touched. This exercise of control and covering was typical for many women in the research. Relatedly, others thought carefully about the places they attended based on how much control they might have in that specific environment. Tai, who is non-binary, spoke of avoiding nights out because of having many times when they were treated as 'an entertainment novelty'. They gave an example of a recent incident where a drunk girl started dancing on their wheelchair. This can then lead to careful consideration about what events might be worth attending. For example, Marina described the way that she would weigh up decisions about travelling each day because of the anticipation of what might happen:

> Being crushed up against, leaned against, shunted along are all agonising. The dilemma of to travel or not to travel is what most disabled people experience daily. Weighing up degrees of pain and its inherent emotional resilience are taken in each journey. Tough one. Just being touched is ghastly. Even the anticipation of it is ghastly.

This dilemma shows that each encounter has the potentiality of being serious and having terrible and diverse impacts. In terms of travelling this is also bound with likely difficulties of having access needs met. Kerry also provided an account of how she manages the exhaustion of moving in public spaces:

> Just navigating the city as a disabled woman comes with a drain of energy, sapping at your self esteem and patience. It has made me shut down parts of my personality that slowly come back through being nice to yourself, and having more awareness to avoid public interaction on the whole, but now I attend more well managed events at accessible places.

These examples show that decisions about daily activities are a careful balancing act for many disabled women. They have to think about access needs and potentially their own skills in avoiding or managing public interaction. These experiences of avoiding or limiting spaces mean that public places are sequestered with disabled women containing their physical presence and their personality. As Vera-Gray and Kelly describe (2020), women's safety work becomes a way of being, not just a way of doing. For disabled women their sense of the embodied self is intrinsically connected with how to be safe in public. This includes gendered and ableist intrusions.

Another familiar aspect of safety work to avoid unwanted ableist intrusions was the use of the male protection racket. This means going out with a male partner or friend, in order to avoid unwanted touching. As previous chapters have shown, this strategy has mixed results but nevertheless can form part of safety planning. Lucy, who detailed her extremely painful reactions to being touched due to allodynia, spoke of how in a busy area she would get her partner to walk directly behind her as protection from people bumping into her. Such was the severity of her pain, she had a negative association with being in crowds. 'If every time you were in that situation someone poked you with a cattle prod, you would no doubt develop the same anxiety over contact by repeated negative reinforcement', she said. Melissa also detailed how the cumulative impact of repeated intrusions had knocked her confidence so that it took many months to rebuild herself to go out and now rarely goes anywhere without her husband. The reliance on partners is dehumanising because they are there to prevent unwanted touching and not to assist with any aspect of accessibility. It further serves to infantilise them and is a visible signifier that disabled women cannot cope alone. Further, it recreates a social environment where women are reliant on men for safety.

For some participants the restriction of personal movements was all-encompassing. Rachel had provided a description of ableist intrusions which showed that they happened a lot to her, almost constantly. It has now gotten to the stage that she won't leave home unaccompanied.

> As a result of these points I rarely leave the house alone, I'm terrified of everyone around me. It worries me greatly that someone could very easily start pushing me in an attempt to kidnap me and get away with it, it would be so easy for them to pose as my 'carer' and the public to ignore my cries for help. It's a massive worry of mine, alongside the daily safety and dignity compromises by being pushed without warning by complete strangers.

'These points' that she refers to are the potential of what might happen, the severity, and also the fact that people ignore her pleas for help. It is this combination of the many facets of ableist intrusions which make them so all-encompassing. It does not necessarily take many incidents for them to have an impact on how disabled women feel. Sarah shared a story whereby even though she had only been a wheelchair user for a year she found that she felt so vulnerable that she would no longer go out alone. Frustrated, she reflected on how previously she would run long distance and so felt capable of dealing with instances of men intruding inappropriately. Now though, things were different:

> I feel that if I was attacked, followed, or had any unwanted attention, I wouldn't be able to get away or avoid it. It would be so easy for anyone to follow me home. I feel trapped.

For many disabled women, feelings of unsafety become more complex when comparing their current experiences to their previous non-disabled life.

ADAPTING SAFETY WORK

A further aspect of safety work for disabled women is the restrictive use of the mobility aid. In earlier chapters it was noted that unwanted touching frequently occurred when people were visibly disabled and that white canes, wheelchairs and guide dogs were signifiers of impairment. They marked out disabled women as 'out of place', particularly in busy settings such as cities or music events and public transport. For this reason, participants often spoke about their attitudes towards their mobility aid. Meena has a chronic illness which means that sometimes she needs to use crutches. She recounted an occasion where a man began shouting at her, using slurs, rape threats and that he was going to hurt her:

> I started walking as fast as I could but knew I wouldn't get to the super-market before he reached me. People walk past looking concerned but no one stops even when I ask. I see a church and there are lights on. I get to the door and get in. As I try to shut the door and lock it the man crashes in on top of me and shouts that he's going to hurt me. Luckily about 4 people run out of the church hall and immediately remove the man from on top of me. They lock him in a room and ask me if I'm ok and if I want to call the police. Someone says that they are going to sit him with some tea and try and calm him down. By this point I'm really crying. I just needed to leave. I know I needed to call the police but all I could do in that moment is leave the church and get onto the first bus away from the situation. I haven't been comfortable using my crutches in public since and the incident happened 5 years ago.

Incidents such as these highlighted what participants frequently talked about in terms of the responses of other strangers and bystanders. Often, onlookers would do nothing at all and in this instance offered the man tea and a chance to calm down. The long-term impacts of incidents such as this can also be noted. Meena's exampled happened five years ago but has resulted in her feeling uncomfortable using her crutches in public as a visible symbol of her disability. Importantly, it is not just the incident of unwanted touching that causes disabled women to adapt their behaviour, but the reaction of bystanders.

Some women in the research expressed not just a caution about using a mobility aid but a deliberate choice over which to use. One example is Emma who describes herself as a lifelong disabled woman who has many experiences of unwanted intrusions which vary depending on the mobility aid she is using. Now a powerchair user, she explained that she avoids using the manual chair in public because it makes her feel less safe. A power chair makes her 'better equipped to cope with the public' because she can use the battery and motors to escape. Other women felt that ableist intrusions made them reflect on the presence of the wheelchair in their lives. For example, Sally uses both an ambulatory wheelchair and an electric bike. When using the bike nobody touches her, but a change in mobility aid makes a huge difference to her daily experiences:

> My wheelchair has expanded my life, but these encounters make me weigh up the pro's and con's every time I consider using it. If I think I can possibly do without it, I will. That really sucks, because it means I end up in more pain and living a smaller life.

This reflection really highlights the impact of cumulative unwanted intrusive behaviours for disabled women. The effect that they have is so significant that the mobility aid which might facilitate their life is something that they might avoid using in order to prevent people from touching them. This was illustrated also by Bess who uses a powerchair. I include the full story here as it describes the multiple layers of her encounter:

> I was within visible distance of my city centre apartment, waiting at the crossing of a main road on my commute, with my headphones in. One of the lesser known symptoms of Chronic Fatigue Syndrome, a disease I've had for almost a decade that has left me using a powered wheelchair, is sensory overload. When out & about music at a controlled volume often helped reduce the overwhelming sounds of a bustling city, & relaxes me ahead of the working day. As I sat watching the traffic flow past, minding my own business, a man who I didn't know bent down so his face was uncomfortably close to mine, leaning over me & invading almost all of my personal space. I pulled out my headphones, which should have been indication enough that I didn't want to make conversation, & was faced with a barrage of insults about how I, as someone with a visible disability, had it easy. He reached into his pocket & my instincts told me to leave as quickly as possible, but where to? There was no way I could dodge

the morning traffic, & I didn't want to give the man any indication of where I lived. He pulled a disabled bus pass from his pocket, waving it around so I couldn't get a name, & began to shout about how he was disabled too even if I couldn't see it, not that I had even challenged that in the first place. The lights turned green & I bolted across the road as he continued to yell at me, & then his apparent friends turned up & joined in. Fortunately, the clamour drew the attention of another man clearly on his way to work, & without making it particularly obvious, he placed himself between me & the men. The men continued to jeer at me but kept their distance, & once we had rounded the corner, the friendly commuter checked that I was alright. The shock kept me from realizing exactly what had happened, so I said yes & continued on my way to work. It was only after putting several locked doors between myself & what had happened that I could even process the situation, & by the time work was done I really didn't want to leave the safety of the medical research centre. I considered putting up my hood & wearing sunglasses, as if somehow that would hide my identity, & maybe taking a different & less accessible route home. However, it being the end of the week I just wanted to get home, & was relieved that nothing happened along the way.

They are dynamic encounters, which might begin when going about their daily business and experiencing a sudden and forceful intrusion. A quick decision has to be made about safety and plans about how to exit the situation which then in turn causes panic and anxiety. Ableist intrusions also might then bring in bystanders who become part of the abuse or might also diffuse the situation. The stories detailed in this research show that each encounter is precarious and unpredictable. But the impact of creating fear and the safety work required is almost constant.

Practical impacts of ableist intrusions clearly demonstrate the way that disabled women might experience pain and harm. The safety work required to counter such situations is significant and has a toll on the well-being and scope of social interactions that they might wish to take part in. Further though, the sense of deep embodiment of these intrusions really can impact on their sense of self and place in the world. Previously we saw that participants spoke of either not responding to unwanted touch or being polite or muted because of the fear of escalation. Anya explained that this was at odds with her personality:

I'm regularly touched by others when using a rollator, but have to ask for things like doors being opened. At work casual acquaintances touch my rollator as I walk by. I felt horribly vulnerable and had to squash my personality when walking around.

This need to be quiet is something Zitzelsberger discusses in her work on (in)visibility and disabled women's accounts of embodiment. As hyper-visible bodies, they cannot escape attention when out in public yet their subjectivities and desires are unseen (2005). To counter this, Anya makes her personality smaller in order to prevent unwanted questions and touch. This has understandable consequences for her sense of self. AJ describes this when reflecting on an incident at a music festival:

I have pretty thick skin and my condition has never stopped me, but the festival incident was different and has left me feeling anxious in big crowds. It made me feel inferior, violated, powerless, scared, knocked my confidence and undermined what I have achieved as a person in spite of my disability. It also made me feel guilty for not using the disabled section at the festival and I now feel like I will have to in future.

Here AJ speaks of the deeper ontological impacts on her as a disabled woman. Cumulative incidents cause a build up of anxiety and fear but also cause an introspective reflection on disability. She feels a sense of achievement in life which is related to her disability—'in spite of'—which is then undermined by unwanted ableist encounters. Alyssa similarly thinks about how each individual act of intrusion is a signifier of so much more than what is happening at that moment. The incident in the lift where she was forcefully touched and then loudly and publicly mocked had a profound impact:

I'll never forget how angry and hopeless I felt, having an elevator full of people side with a man who touched me without consent and laugh at me for trying to defend myself, and not being able to do a thing about it. I'll never forget the realization that I can expect everyone to laugh at me and no one to support me when I am harassed in public. There is nothing I can do to force people to see me as a human being and respect my boundaries. It is hell.

The feeling of hopelessness and realisation of mocking is explained clearly by Alyssa. Participants in this study detailed that there is a frustrating acceptance that intrusions will happen again and no strategy will prevent it. They are robbed of their agency in this moment and note that no safety work will ever make them safe from the ableist touching and objectification of others.

The deep personal impacts of unwanted intrusions place the disabled body in the position of being out of place and labelled with negative stereotypes. To intrude on someone without their permission, or to ignore their requests to be left alone is a persistent act of power play. Denisha describes feeling robbed of her independence and agency. The consequences of unwanted ableist intrusions fundamentally contribute to a loss of autonomy for disabled women, a decrease in their quality of life and chance to contribute fully to citizenship. It cuts to the core of who they are and who they feel they are, impacting on self-confidence and 'frustrating their goals of independent mobility' (Worth, 2013). This is articulated particularly succinctly by Elle:

> I usually feel empowered as a young, Deaf, and fiercely independent woman living in London. I love my work as a professional musician, I have a great group of friends and an amazing fiance, and I enjoy campaigning for greater Deaf awareness in my free time. The only problem is that I suffer from severe anxiety, exacerbated by the public harassment I often endure at the hands of strangers.

The jarring juxtaposition of a young woman describing her joy and vibrancy in life is in stark contrast to the language she uses to detail the behaviour she 'endures', quite literally in the hands of strangers. In Nancy Mair's writing she details the way that disabled women have a journey to go on, one that takes them back to their body but it is hard fought because it 'means finding a place for that body in a misogynist and ableist culture' (Rohrer, 2005, p. 52). The impact of these intrusions is to bring disabled women back to a version of the self and the body that they do not recognise.

References

Edwards, C., & Maxwell, N. (2021). Disability, hostility and everyday geographies of un/safety. *Social & Cultural Geography, 24*(1), 157–174. https://doi.org/10.1080/14649365.2021.1950823

Rohrer, J. (2005). Toward a full-Inclusion feminism: A feminist deployment of disability analysis. *Feminist Studies, 31*(1), 34–63.

Vera-Gray, F., & Kelly, L. (2020). Contested gendered space: Public sexual harassment and women's safety work. *International Journal of Comparative and Applied Criminal Justice, 44*(4), 265–275. https://doi.org/10.1080/01924036.2020.1732435

Wayland, S., Newland, J., Gill-Atkinson, L., Vaughan, C., Emerson, E., & Llewellyn, G. (2020). 'I had every right to be there': Discriminatory acts towards young people with disabilities on public transport. *Disability & Society, 37*(2), 296–319. https://doi.org/10.1080/09687599.2020.1822784

Worth, N. (2013). Visual impairment in the city: Young people's social strategies for independent mobility. *Urban Studies., 50*(3), 574–586. https://doi.org/10.1177/0042098012468898

Zitzelsberger, H. (2005). (In)visibility: Accounts of embodiment of women with physical disabilities and differences. *Disability & Society, 20*(4), 389–403. https://doi.org/10.1080/09687590500086492

CHAPTER 7

Inclusive Not Intrusive

Abstract This chapter draws together the behaviours that define and explain the ableist intrusions that shape the lives of many disabled women. In gathering their narratives, this study has shown that they undertake significant safety work to avoid unwanted touching in public space. Further, this chapter underlines the evident connection between stereotypes of disability and gender and the way that strangers feel entitled to intrude on disabled women's bodies. This chapter also situates this study as a bridge between disability studies and feminist criminology and points towards the importance of scholarship in this area.

Keywords Ableist intrusion · Embodiment · Feminist disability studies · Gender · Intersectionality

DEFINING ABLEIST INTRUSIONS

This sort of thing has happened so many times that I almost barely register it anymore. Since this project was announced until now I have been trying to remember a specific incident, because so many of them blur into one.

H. Mason-Bish, *Disability, Gender, Bodies and Boundaries*, Palgrave Hate Studies, https://doi.org/10.1007/978-3-031-85890-1_7

Danielle's description of the ubiquity of unwanted touch does in fact lead to her describing people tapping her on the head; grabbing her shoulder; having an older man grab her 'rear' to boost her onto a bus and a woman pulling her bag aggressively to 'help' her balance. Women's experiences of unwanted intrusions may be routine but they are also remembered. In Burch's (2021) work on everyday hostility towards disabled people she describes how disability hate crime is both ordinary and extraordinary. Individual incidents have significant impacts, even if they are built into the lives of disabled people. This book has told disabled women's stories in order to identify connections across experiences and to develop deeper understandings of how ableism and sexism intersect and how this is embodied. In this concluding chapter I will draw together the behaviours that define ableist intrusions, their ubiquity and harm. I will further examine the potential motivations of strangers and how these might be seen as a type of ableist anxiety, a performative act which seeks to put the disabled body into the 'correct context'. Finally, I will show how disabled women 'trade freedom for safety' (Vera-Gray, 2018) and underline the way that this book has incorporated the often dismissed voices of disabled women in criminological and feminist research.

This book has developed the concept of ableist intrusions to name the problem of unwanted touching experienced by disabled people. First noted by Calder-Dawe et al. (2019), ableist intrusions start because of the cultural and physical hypervisibility of disabled bodies. The narrow range of bodies which are acceptable in public space means that disabled women are 'highly seen' and more likely to experience intrusive behaviours (Zitzelsberger, 2005). Mobility aids and bodily movements signify disability to non-disabled people and provide the entry point for unwanted touching. Although intrusions have a routine nature, they have a disruptive effect because women do not know when, where or how they might occur. Participants in this book describe how they have a jolting effect, and frequently used the word 'grab' to denote this sudden physical incursion. They also used the words push, lift or squeeze as descriptors of the nature of unwanted touch. In other situations, women were leant on or had their mobility aid used as somewhere for people to hang a bag or coat. This had a similar feeling of being objectified, with their mobility aid being something to assist a stranger. Most of these encounters were silent, very few intruders offered comment or question, let alone sought the consent of the person being touched. The disabled women in the study described having their autonomy removed by these encounters and how they served to remind them of their place in society.

This book also notes how verbal questioning and comments form a significant part of the continuum of behaviours that disabled women experience. Questions were often framed around incompetence, such as asking why they might be out alone or if they were lost. Other insults focused on their perceived attractiveness, for example, people might suggest that the disabled woman was too attractive to be in a wheelchair. Mobility aids undermine a woman's 'visibility as a sexual subject' (Calder-Dawe et al., 2019, p. 144). These forms of questioning demonstrate the way that disabled women experience the 'ordinary interruptions' that Vera-Gray (2017) has written about, but with a confused mix of sexism and ableism. The surprise that disabled women are out in public and looking attractive is seen as something worthy of comment. But it is also about control and the way that disabled women's bodies are relentlessly regulated (Garland-Thomson, 2002).

A key contribution of this book is in demonstrating the nuanced way that gender and disability intersect in particular aspects of intrusive behaviour. Often, the focal point of the interruption was on the mobility aid. For example, wheelchair users described how strangers would move them out of the way. Bal explained that 'wheeling myself is a big part of my independence...an extension of me', demonstrating the embodiment felt by many participants in relation to what their mobility aid meant. Further, intrusions such as this often focused on capacity and compe-tence, with strangers questioning the ability of disabled women to operate their device. While other research has discovered this phenomenon, the intersection of gender and disability is of significance here (see Calder-Dawe et al., 2019; Edwards & Maxwell, 2023). Ableist ejaculations took the form of questions and jokes about the mobility aid were common and drew on gendered themes (see Laniya's, 2005, discussion of verbal ejaculations). The idea that women cannot operate machinery or follow directions and maps entwines with the assumption that disabled people are inherently in need of help. This combination makes up the tone of many intrusive experiences for disabled women and draws a boundary between them and the competent, able-bodied stranger.

This book has also demonstrated the importance of taking an intersec-tional approach to understanding street harassment and stranger intru-sions. Often overlooked by mainstream feminist scholarship, the stories of disabled women show the potentiality of ableist intrusions to escalate to sexual violence and that this ran as an undercurrent through their daily experiences. Sometimes an encounter might begin as an offer of help but shift in tone to become something more sinister. Genevieve described an incident at an airport where she declined the assistance of a ramp agent and he dumped her out of her wheelchair and groped her breasts. Gaia explained the way a man on a train sat near her and touched her legs while making sexually explicit comments. In these cases and many others, a common theme was that when women told people what had happened they were dismissed as misunderstanding or being confused. This dismissal of women making claims about sexual abuse is a common cultural narrative, but for disabled women their disability and bodily self is used as a key part of this denial. It is their disabled body that renders them as unsexual beings (Garland-Thomson, 2001; Santos & Santos, 2018). The fear of escalation combined with the knowledge that they will not be believed is a key part of the way that ableist intrusions operate in the lives of disabled women. They function in a structure of gendered and ableist order and can be a preamble to rape (Gardner, 1995).

AVOIDING INTRUSIONS: THE SAFETY WORK OF DISABLED WOMEN

In gathering the stories of participants, this book has provided a powerful account of the physical and psychological harm that result from intrusive behaviours towards disabled women. While hate crime scholarship has provided rich descriptions of the accumulative impact of hate incidents, this is not often connected with intersectional experiences or broader continuums of abuse (Healy, 2024). This research has shown how seemingly benign encounters cause harm. Participants spoke of bruising, pain, scratches and other physical damage because of strangers touching them without their consent. Often this was the result of people interfering with their mobility aid and putting them in harms way. Sometimes it was because the intrusion came at a moment of concentration such as getting onto a train or crossing a road. There were times when participants requested help but people did not listen in terms of how to give assistance, even when it was being verbally expressed. Injury resulted from not listening and assuming they lacked capacity to understand their own needs. Psychological harms ranged from depression and anxiety to anger and frustration. In the moment of intrusion the women in the study were suddenly and unexpectedly embodying their disability. They were 'brought back' to their body and reminded of what their presence represented in public space. Garland-Thomson speaks of this as a combined management of the body, whereby disabled people must contend with the physical nature of the impairment in spaces not designed to be accessible and the social management of the body in terms of their interactions with strangers (Garland-Thomson, 2014). This has an exhausting impact on their sense of self.

Significantly, this book has addressed a research gap by illuminating the complicated safety work that disabled women undertake to avoid being touched. In assessing their daily movements this involves their choice of clothing or whether to be accompanied by someone as a form of protection. Adaptations to their behaviour though have significant impacts because they often centred around their mobility aid. In removing or adjusting the mobility aid, participants were trying to minimise the chance of being seen as disabled women. The idea that women trade freedom for safety (Vera-Gray, 2018) has quite a particular meaning for some disabled women for whom mobility aids are literal mechanisms of freedom but also the locus of intrusions. Vera-Gray and Kelly (2020) wrote of the way that women perform this kind of adjustment to ensure safety:

> If a woman's body is unsafe in the world, and the risk is understood as not only being in the world but in *the body itself*, then reducing the risk means reducing the body. Instead of clothing then, the adaption here is to women's embodiment: a feeling of (or desire to be) smaller and less visible in the world. (p. 270)

Disabled women's bodies are seen but not heard as their capacity and verbalised rejection of intrusion are ignored. Removing the mobility aid is to make the body less visible. More than that, the women in this study also made themselves and their personalities smaller. Sally spoke of how her life was opened up when she got her wheelchair but the intrusions of others have made her 'live a smaller life'. Kerry has 'shut down parts of [her] personality'. Sarah reflects on an old life as a long distance runner, contrasted with the feeling of entrapment she has now as a wheelchair user because of the unwanted attention that she cannot avoid. These attempts to shrink and hide were at odds with how they felt about themselves. Siobhan said how the intrusions are annoying because she just wants the person gone so she can continue with her day and doesn't 'want or need your ableist pity'. Aisha wants to 'move through the world at my own pace'. Essentially, the safety work for many disabled women involves an alteration of their character which is at odds with the personality and identity that they have cultivated. It 'brings them back to their body' and reduces them to it (Leder, 1990).

ABLEIST ANXIETY AND 'HELP'

While empirical research has noted the role of enforced unwanted assistance in the interactions between disabled people and strangers, this book has demonstrated the importance of understanding this intersectionally (Calder-Dawe et al., 2019; Edwards & Maxwell, 2021; Wayland et al., 2020). 'I was only trying to help' is a frequent theme which runs throughout the stories of the women in this study. I suggest that this statement is the ableist version of 'it was just a compliment' which has come to define women's experiences of catcalling, wolf whistling and street harassment. Both statements share an entitlement to intrude and to read and comment on the bodies of women in public. They also happen after the intrusion, they are not consensual and they lead to an escalation and hostility if rebuked. Neira explained how they operate on an 'assumption that people can only ever have good intentions towards us and those good intentions are more important than anything else, including our agency'. Unwanted intrusions cast as 'help gone wrong' maintain an asymmetric power relationship and firms up the boundaries between disabled and non-disabled people. In loudly and performatively claiming benevolence, the stranger is drawing on well known stereotypes of disabled people as pitiful, vulnerable and weak (Hughes, 2012; Shakespeare, 1994). A refusal of forced help therefore casts the disabled woman as ungrateful but is also a form of public shaming for the person doing the touching. The sudden shift from saviour to aggressor is a reminder that benevolence is conditional and can quickly be withdrawn. This is not to say that people always have malevolent intent when they try to help. But the swift change to hostility demonstrates the need for approval from others as part of the power dynamic of help. It is particularly the case for disabled women as they are more likely to be seen as incapable and in need of assistance.

Simplican (2017) writes of 'ableist anxiety' as a concept to explain non-disabled people's fear of becoming disabled and I have shown how this can be adapted to the intrusions detailed in this book. To encounter disabled people is to expose the vulnerabilities of non-disabled strangers and to bring that into sharp focus. A disabled woman being an active doer, moving in the social world, has a disruptive effect and so something must be done to return to the 'normal' order of things (Loja et al., 2012; Papadimitriou, 2008). That is why participants spoke of interruptions when they were in the physical act of doing something that required a basic element of skill such as using public transport. A common theme in this book was that men would use physical dominance as a part of their intrusion and particularly to comment on the lack of skill that a disabled woman possessed in using a mobility aid. And this intention was hard to discern, particularly as it might be forced help but might also be sexual assault. Both display the ableist and sexist entitlement to touch and the weakness of the female body which requires regulation. Hughes' (2012) discussion of benevolence explains how people convert pity to social capital which is actually 'saturated with selfishness because it sustains ones sense of ontological security' (2012, p. 70). When intrusions are interrupted by an assertive voice this leads to anger and frustration.

This research revealed a very under investigated aspect of stranger interactions—the way that non-disabled women intruded in performative ways. They grabbed, they pushed, they shoved and leant on disabled women. They asked intrusive questions. Some participants described it as a 'mother knows best energy' which speaks again to the infantilising of disabled women and their assumed lack of capacity. In a small study such as this it is difficult to draw out motivations but further research on the gendered nature of intrusive practices is warranted. It is likely they are similarly 'converting pity to social capital' (Hughes, 2012) and doing so in a loud and expressive way. However, a note on the limits of this project might demonstrate future avenues to explore this. Due to a lack of demographic data it is not possible to be sure about the race and age of participants. It is likely that black and minority ethnic women experience different and more sexually aggressive intrusions as has been evidenced in intersectional accounts of street harassment (Davis, 1993; Fogg-Davis, 2006). Similarly, research on young disabled people shows that they find it hard to be seen as competent members of society because of interruptions by strangers (Worth, 2013). There are interesting questions to be asked about the way that non-disabled women view their own bodies and capacity and to a similar extent the female body is never truly valued (Wendell, 1996). There are in fact very few bodies which can 'maintain a physical presence in public space without social challenge' (Butler &

Bowlby, 1997, p. 420). How this dynamic translates into the intrusive behaviours of women towards other women is an area for future research.

THE CONTINUUM OF ABLEIST INTRUSIONS

Amy Kavanagh has described the jarring and deep embodiment that happens when she is intruded upon by a stranger. When she first went out using her white cane she found that there was a 'fundamental disconnect between my joy in my disabled self and the reactions of non-disabled people' (Kavanagh, 2022). For disabled women the body therefore dysappears as they are not allowed to be socially competent actors. Instead they must play along or think carefully about their response for fear of escalation. In the moment of touch they become an emblem of a disabled body, noted and needing to be grabbed. In this way 'disability is experienced in, on and through the body, just as impairment is experienced in terms of the personal and cultural narratives that help to constitute its meaning' (Hughes & Paterson, 1997, pp. 334–335). These impacts can be so serious because intentions can be plausibly denied. Just as 'it was only a compliment' is a believable riposte to a catcall, 'I was only trying to help' has a similar effect. This study did not look at disabled men who also experience regular unwanted intrusions and it is important that future research does incorporate their experiences. However, there are particular nuances at the intersection of gender and disability that have been uncovered by this research. Ableist intrusions are the way that asymmetrical relations are maintained and enacted. They sit at the intersection of chivalry and charity meaning that strangers intrude on disabled women and disrupt the flow of their daily lives. The disabled female body is particularly viewed as lacking capacity and being in a constant state of weakness. The safety work they undertake is based partly on the assessment of whether unwanted touching has a sexual intention.

The intrusions discussed in this book provide a valuable contribution to feminist criminology as they are an important part of the continuum of abuse and violence that disabled women experience across the life course. Participant Lisa I provided a story which I include here in full as she details the way that ableist violence has punctuated her life, how it has 'chipped away at her essence' and how she would like her consent and autonomy to be valued.

I ask that you please post my story on my behalf. Please include my actual name, Lisa I. My adversities have helped me to become a strong, compassionate woman who holds hope when others have lost it, or don't believe hope exists anymore.

Decades ago I began to search for information about my adoption. I recall finding a letter from the adoption attorney who commended my adoptive mother for taking on the "Burdon" of caring for a "handicapped" child. Fifty years later some of those perceptions have not changed much. The first time I grasped that a stranger was cutting me with his words was when I was maybe nine years old. I don't recall the specifics of what the grown man said to me but I remember understanding that he was putting me down because I was blind. Similar scenarios have played out and taken their toll on my spirit, chipping but not eroding my essence. Here are just a few more examples of cruel words and ableist attitudes that have imprinted themselves within my inner-being. A college music professor, told me how helpless I looked using my cane. An " ex" told me to, "put that thing away". (He meant my cane). For a while I did hide my cane because I just wanted to blend in but I never blended in.

In the late 1980s a nursing home administrator who I worked for called me into her office. She privately told me that she was not going to give me "special treatment". She went on to tell me that she would never have hired me because of my very thick glasses. Twenty years later I met up with the former administrator at an adult education class. I wanted so much to confront her but I figured she'd likely not remember, or she'd deny her ableist and heartless attitude and words.

Let's talk about intrusive touches. A few encounters really stand out. For starters, in the mid-1970s, I left the nearby school for the blind and started seventh grade at the nearby public school. I recall standing in the front office and in walked a Special Education teacher who proceeded to put her hands on the frames of my glasses and attempted to remove them from my face. I resisted. Her words stung the insecure adolescent who just wanted to fit in at her new school. The teacher trained to help students with disabilities spoke past me and said, "feisty creature!" I wasn't even human! I didn't have autonomy over my developing body according to this college educated professional.

Fast-forward thirty years. I and my elementary school age son were at a cross walk waiting to cross the street. A man came up from up behind me and grabbed my arm. I screamed. I yelled for him to get his hand off of me. Of course, he self-justified his actions. I countered that I had no clue what his intentions were. I told him something to the effect that his intentions could have been to rape me. He screamed back, "who would want to rape you!" (Actually, 85% of disabled women are victims of sexual assault or rape).His inference was that I wasn't a sexual being. I guess the stork really did deliver my son.

More recently, about several years ago I was back in the dating scene. I was interested in a well-rounded, educated and spiritual grounded man I met at church. I concluded real fast that he didn't view me as his equal after one particular demeaning and hurtful encounter. I had asked for directions out of the worship center. This man who worked with acutely ill individuals and had a background in divinity came up from behind me; placed his hands on my shoulders and propelled and manipulated my body out of the sanctuary. I wasn't a woman in his eyes; I was an object without consideration for emotions, feelings or relationships. On a more humorous note, I later discovered that he was already engaged. Lol.

Over the past few years I've become more vocal and more assertive when misguided folks opt to use their hands rather than their words. Contrary to the woman at a San Diego bank who vehemently disagreed when I informed her that I was her equal; I am and that will not change. Therefore, my body is mine and no one touches my body without my consent.

Lisa's story shows how it is not possible to consider her experiences of intrusion in isolation. They are part of the contours of her daily life and form a frame through which she knows the world.

Inclusive Not Intrusive

The findings in this research are an entry point to what should be a growing body of academic scholarship. This book has taken up Garland-Thomson's challenge that disability must be integrated as a category of inquiry within feminist research (Garland-Thomson, 2002, p. 28). Neglected also by criminology, the focus on the lived experiences of disabled women demonstrates that they are best placed to discuss the unwanted behaviours that happen to them. In considering the intersection of gender and disability, the voices of trans and non-binary groups need to be part of the story. With rising rates of transphobic rhetoric, it unfortunately follows that bodies seen as out of place are more likely to be targeted for a range of abuse and intrusive behaviours (Home Office, 2023). Transgender and non-binary adults are more likely to be disabled and/or experience long-term illness than cisgender people (Saunders et al., 2023; Smith-Johnson, 2022). Research examining the compound oppressions at the intersection of disability and gender identity is therefore of timely importance (Baril & Silverman, 2022; Baril et al., 2020). I have not avoided a 'white feminist approach to ableism' (More, 2023, p. 332), so further work must incorporate a variety of voices and lessons from both Black feminist scholarship and activism (Schalk, 2020). Indeed to avoid 'lazy intersectionality' other diverse and under-studied groups of disabled people should make up future research because they share ableist intrusive practices (Watermeyer & Swartz, 2022). More scholarship is needed recognising the role of class, the rural/urban nature of space and also to incorporate a broad range of impairments including learning disabilities. Academia can learn from the vital work of disability activists who have not been quiet about the types of behaviour that I have detailed. Attending to their narratives and providing inclusive spaces for this dialogue to happen, is a central part of attempting to break down the ableist barriers in academia and wider society.

Being a non-disabled woman I have attempted to tread a careful path of allyship and to use my academic privilege to 'pass the mic'. As such, it is only appropriate to conclude by highlighting what the participants in the study hoped would change as a result of sharing their stories. First is a greater awareness of consent. Participant Denisha explains this:

> One positive experience I had was two winters ago when the streets were really icy and I was having a very hard time collecting my shopping. A young woman saw me struggling up the hill and asked if I needed any help. At that point, I really did. She held out her arm for me to take, which was exactly the right thing to do, and offered to carry some of my shopping for me. She was a trainee social worker and had a really good understanding of how to offer help in a way that was empowering. We actually had a good chat about the power dynamics of offering help on our way up the hill. I was very grateful that she stopped to help me that day.

This research project is not about ignoring disabled women and it is not about denying them help. In Denisha's story she details a number of instances of unwanted touching including rape, aggressive 'manhandling' and abuse that 'rob her of her independence'. In this example, the help was offered verbally and consent was sought before any physical touch. Instead of being seen as public property that strangers can 'paw at', she says that she does not mind people asking or offering help 'but I need them to listen when I say I'm fine'. The verbal offer and consideration of consent transforms the encounter and transforms Denisha from an object to a subject, with her own capacity and agency. The role of agency and independence was a central and repeated theme in the participant stories. Connected to this was a hope that people would listen and believe what was happening to them. In many of the stories of sexual assault, harassment and abuse, strangers would look away or deny what was happening. This built-in assumption that no one would find a disabled woman attractive was often used during verbal and physical abuse. As Cerise describes, people assume that she should be 'flattered because society views us disabled people as non sexual / non desirable'. Participants hoped that people would understand the power dynamics at play. Issues of consent and believability were connected to what many described as just being treated as a human being. The glimpses of joy and hope for change and fulfilment were detailed throughout the stories. Kerry spoke of the way that since beginning to drive she is able to control the number of inappropriate interactions and so has 'far more energy to focus on my goals, life and my interests'. She can participate in society, having the time and confidence to do so.

Finally, an abiding request was to be allowed to move through the world without ableist, gendered intrusion. Whether a stranger trying to 'help'; a physical assault or someone asking an ableist question, participants in this project wanted privacy, safety and to navigate public space without interruption. The behaviour of strangers had a destabilising effect, highlighting disability as something out of place and requiring intervention. In understanding a concept of ableist intrusion it is hoped that society can appreciate the right of disabled women to occupy public space. The final word on this comes from Alaya, who articulately sums up what encounters with the public should be like:

> People should use their words instead of their hands. People should accept 'no' without getting in their feelings...Think before you speak, ask before you touch, truly listen to responses and be willing to grow past bias and misconceptions. It really is that simple.

REFERENCES

Burch, L. (2021). *Understanding disability and everyday hate*. Palgrave Macmillan.

Baril, A., Sansfaçon, A. P., & Gelly, M. A. (2020). Digging beneath the surface: When disability meets gender identity. *Canadian Journal of Disability Studies, 9*, 1–23.

Baril, A., & Silverman, M. (2022). Forgotten lives: Trans older adults living with dementia at the intersection of cisgenderism, ableism/cogniticism and ageism. *Sexualities, 25*(1–2), 117–131.

Butler, R., & Bowlby, S. (1997). Bodies and spaces: An exploration of disabled people's experiences of public space. *Environment and Planning D: Society and Space, 15*(4), 411–433. https://doi.org/10.1068/d150411

Calder-Dawe, O., Witten, K., & Carroll, P. (2019). Being the body in question: Young people's accounts of everyday ableism, visibility and disability. *Disability & Society, 35*, 132–155.

Davis, D. E. (1993). The harm that has no name: Street harassment, embodiment, and African American women. *UCLA Women's Law Journal*.

Edwards, C., & Maxwell, N. (2021). Disability, hostility and everyday geographies of un/safety. *Social & Cultural Geography, 24*(1), 157–174. https://doi.org/10.1080/14649365.2021.1950823

Edwards, C., & Maxwell, N. (2023). Troubling ambulant research: Disabled people's socio-spatial encounters with urban un/safety and the politics of mobile methods. *Irish Journal of Sociology, 31*(1) 63–81. https://doi.org/10.1177/07916035221098601

Fogg-Davis, H. G. (2006). Theorizing Black lesbians within Black feminism: A critique of same-race street harassment. *Politics & Gender, 2*(1), 57–76. https://doi.org/10.1017/S1743923X06060028

Garland-Thomson, R. (2001). Re-shaping, re-thinking, re-defining: Feminist disability studies. *The Barbara Waxman Fiduccia Papers on Women and Girls with Disabilities*. Washington DC: Center for Women Policy Studies. https://bpb-us-e2.wpmucdn.com/sites.middlebury.edu/dist/1/4371/files/2020/03/Garland-Thomson_Redefining_Feminist_Disabilities_Studies_2001.pdf

Garland-Thomson, R. (2002a). Integrating disability, transforming feminist theory. *NWSA Journal, 14*(3), 1–32.

Garland-Thomson, R. (2014). The story of my work: How I became disabled. *Disability Studies Quarterly, 34*(2).

Gardner, C. B. (1995). *Passing by: Gender and public harassment*. University of California Press.

Healy, J. (2024). Revealing the benefits, barriers, and prevalence of intersectionality in disability hate crime research. In L. Burch, & D. Wilkin (Eds.), *Disability hate crime: Perspectives for change*. Routledge.

Home Office. (2023). *Hate crime statistics.* https://www.gov.uk/government/statistics/hate-crime-england-and-wales-2022-to-2023/hate-crime-england-and-wales-2022-to-2023

Hughes, B. (2012). Fear, pity and disgust: Emotions and the non-disabled imaginary. In N. Watson, A. Roulstone & C. Thomas (Eds). *Routledge handbook of disability studies* (1st ed., pp. 67–78). Routledge.

Hughes, B., & Paterson, K. (1997). The social model of disability and the disappearing body: Toward a sociology of impairment. *Disability & Society, 12*(3), 325–340.

Kavanagh, A. (2022). *Hands off: Navigating unwanted touch, consent and disability.* University of Oxford Annual Disability Lecture [Transcript]. Retrieved November 1, 2024 from https://podcasts.ox.ac.uk/2022-disability-lecture-hands-navigating-unwanted-touch-consent-and-disability

Laniya, O. O. (2005). Street smut: Gender, media, and the legal power dynamics of street harassment, or hey sexy and other verbal ejaculations. *Columbia Journal of Gender and Law, 14*(1), 91–142.

Leder, D. (1990). *The absent body.* University of Chicago Press.

Loja, E., Costa, M. E., Hughes, B., & Menezes, I. (2012). Disability, embodiment and ableism: Stories of resistance. *Disability & Society, 28*(2), 190–203. https://doi.org/10.1080/09687599.2012.705057

More, R. (2023). Storying ableism: Proposing a feminist intersectional approach to linking theory and digital activism. *Feminist Theory, 25*(3), 322–337. https://doi.org/10.1177/14647001231173242

Papadimitriou, C. (2008). 'It was hard but you did it': The co-production of 'work' in a clinical setting among spinal cord injured adults and their physical therapists. *Disability & Rehabilitation, 30*(5), 365–374.

Santos, A. C., & Santos, A. L. (2018). Yes, we fuck! Challenging the misfit sexual body through disabled women's narratives. *Sexualities, 21*(3), 303–318. https://doi.org/10.1177/1363460716688680

Saunders, C. L., et al. (2023, February). Demographic characteristics, long-term health conditions, and healthcare experiences of 6,333 trans and non-binary adults in England: Nationally representative evidence from the 2021 GP Patient Survey. *BMJ Open.* https://doi.org/10.1136/bmjopen-2022-068099

Schalk, S. (2020). Contextualizing black disability and the culture of dissemblance. *Signs, 45*(3), 535–540.

Shakespeare, T. (1994). Cultural representation of disabled people: Dustbins for disavowal? *Disability and Society, 9*(3), 283–299. https://doi.org/10.1080/09687599466780341

Simplican, S. C. (2017). Feminist disability studies as methodology: Life-writing and the abled/disabled binary. *Feminist Review, 115*(1), 46–60.

Smith-Johnson, M. (2022). Transgender adults have higher rates of disability than their cisgender counterparts. *Health Affairs, 41*(10), 1470–1476.

Vera-Gray, F. (2017). *Men's Intrusion, Women's Embodiment: A Critical Analysis of Street Harassment*. Routledge.

Vera-Gray, F. (2018). *The right amount of panic: How women trade freedom for safety in public*. Policy Press.

Vera-Gray, F., & Kelly, L. (2020). Contested gendered space: Public sexual harassment and women's safety work. *International Journal of Comparative and Applied Criminal Justice, 44*(4), 265–275. https://doi.org/10.1080/01924036.2020.1732435

Watermeyer, B., & Swartz, L. (2022). Disability and the problem of lazy intersectionality. *Disability & Society, 38*(2), 362–366. https://doi.org/10.1080/09687599.2022.2130177

Wayland, S., Newland, J., Gill-Atkinson, L., Vaughan, C., Emerson, E., & Llewellyn, G. (2020). I had every right to be there: Discriminatory acts towards young people with disabilities on public transport. *Disability & Society, 37*(2), 296–319. https://doi.org/10.1080/09687599.2020.1822784

Wendell, S. (1996). *The rejected body. Feminist philosophical reflections on disability*. Routledge.

Worth, N. (2013). Visual impairment in the city: Young people's social strategies for independent mobility. *Urban Studies., 50*(3), 574–586. https://doi.org/10.1177/0042098012468898

Zitzelsberger, H. (2005). (In)visibility: Accounts of embodiment of women with physical disabilities and differences. *Disability & Society, 20*(4), 389–403. https://doi.org/10.1080/09687590500086492

FURTHER READING

About Access. (2019). *Wheelchair spikes make the point about unwanted help.* [Online] Retrieved September 4, 2024 from https://aboutaccess.co.uk/whe elchair-spikes-make-the-point-about-unwanted-help/

Acker-Verney, J. M. (2016). Embedding intersectionality and reflexivity in research: Doing accessible and inclusive research with persons with disabilities. *Third World Thematics: A TWQ Journal, 1*(3), 411–424. https://doi. org/10.1080/23802014.2016.1235468

Ahlvik-Harju, C. (2016). Disturbing bodies—Reimagining comforting narratives of embodiment through feminist disability studies. *Scandinavian Journal of Disability Research, 18*(3), 222–233. https://doi.org/10.1080/15017419. 2015.1063545

Arzroomchilar, E. (2024). Why disability is technologically mediated? *Human Studies.* https://doi.org/10.1007/s10746-024-09722-9

Balderston, S. (2013a). After disablist hate crime: Which interventions really work to resist victimhood and build resilience with survivors? In A. Roulstone & H. Mason-Bish (Eds.), *Disability, hate crime and violence* (pp. 177–192). Routledge.

Balderston, S. (2013b). Victimised again? Intersectionality and injustice in disabled women's lives after hate crime and rape. In M. Texler Segal, & V. Demos (Eds.), *Gendered perspectives on conflict and violence: Part A.* Advances in Gender Research, Volume 18A (pp. 17–51). Emerald Group Publishing Ltd.

Balderston, S. (2014). *Surviving disablist hate rape: Barriers, intersectionalities and collective interventions with disabled women in the North of England* (Doctoral Thesis, Lancaster University). Lancaster University.

Barbarin, I. (2018). Disabled people have an ally problem: They need to stop talking for us. *Crutches and Spice* [Online]. Retrieved October 11, 2024, from https://crutchesandspice.com/2018/05/15/disabled-people-have-an-ally-problem-they-need-to-stop-talking-for-us/

Baril, A., Sansfaçon, A. P., & Gelly, M. A. (2020). Digging beneath the surface: When disability meets gender identity. *Canadian Journal of Disability Studies*, 9, 1–23.

Baril, A., & Silverman, M. (2022). Forgotten lives: Trans older adults living with dementia at the intersection of cisgenderism, ableism/cogniticism and ageism. *Sexualities*, 25(1–2), 117–131.

Barnes, C., & Mercer, G. (1997). Breaking the mould? An introduction to doing disability research. In C. Barnes & G. Mercer (Eds.), *Doing disability research* (pp. 1–14). Disability Press.

Barnes, C. (1996). Disability and the myth of the independent researcher. *Disability & Society*, 11(2), 107–110.

Bates, L. (2015). *Everyday sexism*. Simon & Shuster.

Bê, A. (2012). Feminism and disability—A cartography of multiplicity. In N. Watson, A. Roulstone & C. Thomas (Eds.), *Routledge handbook of disability studies* (pp. 363–375). Taylor & Francis.

Beckwith, D., & Drake, G. (2022). Exploring women's experiences of sexuality education, sexual expression and violence: Inclusive research with disabled women. *Disability & Society*, 39(2), 422–434. https://doi.org/10.1080/096 87599.2022.2071677

Berg, B. [@bergbronwyn]. (2019, January 13). *If you see a person in a wheelchair (especially a woman) being pushed by someone and she's screaming Stop! No! [Post]*. Twitter. https://twitter.com/bergbronwyn/status/108424 0379535392769

Berger, R. J. (2013). *Introducing disability studies*. Lynne Reiner Publishers.

Blakely, K. (2007). Reflections on the role of emotion in feminist research. *International Journal of Qualitative Methods*, 6(2), 59–68. https://doi.org/10. 1177/160940690700600206

Bowman, C. (1993). Street harassment and the informal ghettoization of women. *Harvard Law Review*, 106(3), 517–580. https://doi.org/10.2307/1341656

Boyer, K. (2022). Sexual harassment and the right to everyday life. *Progress in Human Geography*, 46(2), 398–415.

Brooks, H. (2021, April 26). *Now that I'm disabled, society does not seem to care about my sexual safety*. Metro (online). Retrieved October 1, 2024 from https://metro.co.uk/2021/04/26/now-im-disabled-society-does-not-seem-to-care-about-my-sexual-safety-14465022/

Brown, L. X. Z. (2017). Ableist shame and disruptive bodies: Survivorship at the intersection of queer, trans, and disabled existence. In A. J. Johnson, J. R. Nelson, & E. M. Lund (Eds.), *Religion, disability, and interpersonal violence* (pp. 163–178). Springer International Publishing/Springer Nature. https:// doi.org/10.1007/978-3-319-56901-7_10

Brown, N., & Leigh, J. (Eds.). (2020). *Ableism in academia: Theorising experiences of disabilities and chronic illnesses in higher education*. UCL Press. https://doi.org/10.14324/111.9781787354975

Burch, L. (2023). 'I haven't got anywhere safe': Disabled people's experiences of hate and violence within the home. *Social & Cultural Geography, 25*(6), 967–984. https://doi.org/10.1080/14649365.2023.2242325

Burch, L. (2024). Working "with" not "on" disabled people: The role of hate crime research within the community. *Journal of Interpersonal Violence, 39*(17–18), 3932–3953. https://doi.org/10.1177/08862605241260005

Burch, L., Hollomotz, A., & Bashall, R. (2023). *Formal support needs of disabled adult victim survivors of sexual violence: A qualitative research report*. Ministry of Justice, London: Crown. https://eprints.whiterose.ac.uk/212132/1/formal-support-needs-of-disabled-adult-victim-survivors-of-sexual-violence-research-report.pdf

Butler, R., & Bowlby, S. (1997). Bodies and spaces: An exploration of disabled people's experiences of public space. *Environment and Planning D: Society and Space, 15*(4), 411–433. https://doi.org/10.1068/d150411

Calder-Dawe, O., Witten, K., & Carroll, P. (2019). Being the body in question: Young people's accounts of everyday ableism, visibility and disability. *Disability & Society, 35*, 132–155.

Calderbank, R. (2000). Abuse and disabled people: Vulnerability or social indifference? *Disability & Society, 15*(3), 521–534. https://doi.org/10.1080/713661966

Campbell, R. (2001). *Emotionally involved: The impact of researching rape* (1st ed.). Routledge.

Chakravarti, U. (2015). A gendered perspective of disability studies. In A. Hans (Ed.), *Disability, gender and trajectories of power*. SAGE Publications.

Cockain, A. (2022). Making spaces in exclusionary places: The spatial tactics/ stories of disabled people and their families in Hong Kong. *Disability & Society, 38*(10), 1913–1933. https://doi.org/10.1080/09687599.2022.2061331

Crenshaw, K. (1991). Mapping the margins: Intersectionality, identity politics, and violence against women of color. *Stanford Law Review, 43*(6), 1241–1299.

Davis, D. E. (1993). The harm that has no name: Street harassment, embodiment, and African American women. *UCLA Women's Law Journal, 4*(2), 133–178.

Edwards, C., & Maxwell, N. (2021). Disability, hostility and everyday geographies of un/safety. *Social & Cultural Geography, 24*(1), 157–174. https:// doi.org/10.1080/14649365.2021.1950823

Edwards, C., & Maxwell, N. (2023). Troubling ambulant research: Disabled people's socio-spatial encounters with urban un/safety and the politics of mobile methods. *Irish Journal of Sociology, 31*(1), 63–81. https://doi.org/10.1177/07916035221098601

Ellis, L. (2017). Through a filtered lens: Unauthorized picture-taking of people with dwarfism in public spaces. *Disability & Society, 33*(2), 218–237. https://doi.org/10.1080/09687599.2017.1392930

Emmett, T., & Alant, E. (2006). Women and disability: Exploring the interface of multiple disadvantage. *Development Southern Africa, 23*(4), 445–460. https://doi.org/10.1080/03768350600927144

Fileborn, B., & Vera-Gray, F. (2017). "I want to be able to walk the street without fear": Transforming justice for street harassment. *Feminist Legal Studies, 25*, 203–227. https://doi.org/10.1007/s10691-017-9350-3

Flores, E. (2018, April 24). The #MeToo movement hasn't been inclusive of the disability community. *Teen Vogue*. Retrieved October 11, 2024 from https://www.teenvogue.com/story/the-metoo-movement-hasnt-been-inclusive-of-the-disability-community

Fontaine, J. (2021). When girls walk: Mobilities of and resistance to affective atmospheres of unwelcome. *Space and Culture, 25*, 633–644.

Gappmayer, G. (2020). Disentangling disablism and ableism: The social norm of being able and its influence on social interactions with people with intellectual disabilities. *Journal of Occupational Science, 28*(1), 102–113. https://doi.org/10.1080/14427591.2020.1814394

Gardner, C. B. (1995). *Passing by: Gender and public harassment*. University of California Press.

Garland-Thomson, R. (2001). *Re-shaping, re-thinking, re-defining: Feminist disability studies* (The Barbara Waxman Fiduccia Papers on Women and Girls with Disabilities). Center for Women Policy Studies. https://bpb-us-e2.wpmucdn.com/sites.middlebury.edu/dist/1/4371/files/2020/03/Garland-Thomson_Redefining_Feminist_Disabilities_Studies_2001.pdf

Garland-Thomson, R. (2002). Integrating disability, transforming feminist theory. *NWSA Journal, 14*(3), 1–32.

Garland-Thomson, R. (2005). Feminist disability studies: A review of essays. *Signs, 30*(2), 1557–1587.

Garland-Thomson, R. (2009) *Staring: How we look*. Oxford and New York: Oxford.

Garland-Thomson, R. (2011). Misfits: A feminist materialist disability concept. *Hypatia: A Journal of Feminist Philosophy, 26*(3), 591–609.

Garland-Thomson, R. (2013). Disability studies: A field emerged. *American Quarterly, 65*(4), 915–926.

Garland-Thomson, R. (2014). The story of my work: How I became disabled. *Disability Studies Quarterly, 34*(2).

Ghosh, N. (2015). Sites of oppression: Dominant ideologies and women with disabilities in India. In T. Shakespeare (Ed.), *Disability research today* (pp. 77–92). Routledge.

Goodley, D., & Lawthom, R. (2019). Critical disability studies, Brexit and Trump: A time of neoliberal–ableism. *Rethinking History, 23*(2), 233–251. https://doi.org/10.1080/13642529.2019.1607476

Hague, G., Thiara, R., & Mullender, A. (2011). Disabled women and domestic violence: Making the links, a national UK study. *Psychiatry, Psychology and Law, 18*(1), 117–136. https://doi.org/10.1080/13218719.2010.509040

Hanisch, H. (2014). Psycho-emotional disablism: A differentiated process. *Scandinavian Journal of Disability Research, 16*(3), 211–228. https://doi.org/10.1080/15017419.2013.795911

Healy, J. (2019a). Thinking outside the box: Intersectionality as a hate crime research framework. *Papers from the British Criminology Conference, 19*, 60–83.

Healy, J. (2019b). 'It spreads like a creeping disease': Experiences of victims of disability hate crimes in austerity Britain. *Disability & Society, 35*(2), 176–200. https://doi.org/10.1080/09687599.2019.1624151

Healy, J. (2022). Examining disability hate crime. In J. Healy, & B. Colliver (Eds.), *Contemporary intersectional criminology in the UK examining the boundaries of intersectionality and crime.* Policy Press.

Healy, J. (2024). Revealing the benefits, barriers, and prevalence of intersectionality in disability hate crime research. In L. Burch, & D. Wilkin (Eds.), *Disability hate crime: Perspectives for change.* Routledge.

Hindes, S., & Fileborn, B. (2023). "Why did he do it? because he's a Fucking Bloke": Victim insights into the perpetration of street harassment. *British Journal of Criminology, 63*(3), 668–686. https://doi.org/10.1093/bjc/azac029

Home Office. (2023). *Hate crime statistics* [online]. Retrieved October 1, 2024 from https://www.gov.uk/government/statistics/hate-crime-england-and-wales-2022-to-2023/hate-crime-england-and-wales-2022-to-2023

Horvath, M. A. H., & Brown, J. M. (Eds.). (2022). *Rape: Challenging contemporary thinking—10 years on* (2nd ed.). Routledge. https://doi.org/10.4324/9781003163800

Houston, E. (2019). 'Risky' representation: The portrayal of women with mobility impairment in twenty-first-century advertising. *Disability & Society, 34*(5), 704–725. https://doi.org/10.1080/09687599.2019.1576505

Hughes, B. (1999). The constitution of impairment: Modernity and the aesthetic of oppression. *Disability & Society, 14*(2), 155–172.

Hughes, B. (2007). Being disabled: Towards a critical social ontology for disability studies. *Disability & Society, 22*(7), 673–684. https://doi.org/10.1080/09687590701659527

Hughes, B. (2009). Wounded/monstrous/abject: A critique of the disabled body in the sociological imaginary. *Disability & Society, 24*, 399–410.

Hughes, B. (2012). Fear, pity and disgust: Emotions and the non-disabled imaginary. In N. Watson, A. Roulstone & C. Thomas (Eds.), *Routledge handbook of disability studies* (1st ed., pp. 67–78). Routledge.

Hughes, B. (2019). The abject and the vulnerable: The twain shall meet: Reflections on disability in the moral economy. *The Sociological Review, 67*(4), 829–846. https://doi.org/10.1177/0038026119854259

Hughes, B., & Paterson, K. (1997). The social model of disability and the disappearing body: Toward a sociology of impairment. *Disability & Society, 12*(3), 325–340.

Imrie, R. F. (1996). *Disability and the city: International perspectives*. Paul Chapman.

Imrie, R. (2004). Disability, embodiment and the meaning of the home. *Housing Studies, 19*(5), 745–763.

Jackson, S., & Scott, S. (2023). Storytelling, sociology and sexuality: Ken Plummer's humanist narrative analysis. *Sexualities, 26*(4), 476–485. https://doi.org/10.1177/13634607231169003

Kavanagh, A. (2022). *Hands off: Navigating unwanted touch, consent and disability*. University of Oxford Annual Disability Lecture [Transcript]. Retrieved October 1, 2024 from https://podcasts.ox.ac.uk/2022-disability-lecture-hands-navigating-unwanted-touch-consent-and-disability.

Kavanagh, A., & Mason-Bish, H. (2019). As a disabled woman, I'm harassed on the street daily—Where's My #MeToo movement? *Huffington Post* [online]. Retrieved October 1, 2024 from https://www.huffingtonpost.co.uk/entry/disabled-woman-me-too_uk_5d3eaee2e4b0db8affaadf12

Keith, L. (1996). Encounters with strangers: The public's responses to disabled women and how this affects our sense of self. In J. Morris (Ed.), *Encounters with strangers: Feminism and disability* (pp. 69–89). The Women's Press.

Kelly, L. (1988). *Surviving sexual violence*. Polity Press.

Kitchin, R. (1998). "Out of place", "knowing one's place": Space, power and the exclusion of disabled people. *Disability & Society, 13*(3), 343–356. https://doi.org/10.1080/09687599826678

Kitchin, R. (2000). The researched opinions on research: Disabled people and disability research. *Disability & Society, 15*(1), 25–47. https://doi.org/10.1080/09687590025757

Kirk-Wade, E., Stiebahl, S., & Wong, H. (2024). *UK disability statistics: Prevalence and life experiences*. Research Briefing, House of Common Library.

Laniya, O. O. (2005). Street smut: Gender, media, and the legal power dynamics of street harassment, or hey sexy and other verbal ejaculations. *Columbia Journal of Gender and Law, 14*(1), 91–142.

Leder, D. (1990). *The absent body*. University of Chicago Press.

Lenney, M., & Sercombe, H. (2002). 'Did you see that guy in the wheelchair down the pub?' Interactions across difference in a public place. *Disability & Society, 17*(1), 5–18. https://doi.org/10.1080/09687590120100093

Lewis, T. (2021, January 1). Working definition of ableism. *Talila Lewis*. Retrieved October 10, 2024, from https://www.talilalewis.com/blog/january-2021-working-definition-of-ableism

Lloyd, M. (1992). Does she boil eggs? Towards a feminist model of disability. *Disability, Handicap & Society, 7*(3), 207–221. https://doi.org/10.1080/02674649266780231

Lin, Z., & Yang, L. (2019). 'Me too!': Individual empowerment of disabled women in the #MeToo movement in China. *Disability & Society, 34*(5), 842–847. https://doi.org/10.1080/09687599.2019.1596608

Lockwood, N., & Scott, S. (2023). Saying something with nothing: Refusal, avoidance and resistance in participant non-response. *Methodological Innovations, 16*(2), 215–225. https://doi.org/10.1177/20597991231179390

Loja, E., Costa, M. E., Hughes, B., & Menezes, I. (2012). Disability, embodiment and ableism: Stories of resistance. *Disability & Society, 28*(2), 190–203. https://doi.org/10.1080/09687599.2012.705057

Love, G., & McDonnell, L. (2024). Presence as politics in qualitative research ethics: Feminist engagements with "risk" and vulnerability. *Qualitative Inquiry*. https://doi.org/10.1177/10778004241256141

Low, H. (2019, October 15). Spikes—And other ways disabled people combat unwanted touching. *BBC Ouch*. Retrieved October 10, 2024 from https://www.bbc.co.uk/news/disability-49584591

Macdonald, S. J., Donovan, C., & Clayton, J. (2021). 'I may be left with no choice but to end my torment': Disability and intersectionalities of hate crime. *Disability & Society, 38*(1), 127–147. https://doi.org/10.1080/09687599.2021.1928480

MacDonald, S. J., & Peacock, D. (2024). Dis/ableist criminology: Applying disability theory within a criminological context. In K. J. Stockdale, & M. Addison (Eds.), *Marginalised voices in criminology* (pp. 13–31). Routledge.

Mairs, N. (1996). *Carnal acts*. Beacon Press.

Mason-Bish, H. (2013). Conceptual issues in the construction of disability hate crime. In A. Roulstone, & H. Mason-Bish (Eds.), *Disability, hate crime and violence* (pp. 11–24). Routledge.

Mason-Bish, H. (2015). Beyond the silo: Rethinking hate crime and intersectionality. In N. Hall, A. Corb, P. Giannasi & J. G. D. Grieve (Eds.), *The Routledge international handbook on hate crime* (pp. 24–33). Routledge.

Mason-Bish, H. (2019, August 26). Disabled women are being constantly groped without their consent—Even by people who think they are helping [Online]. *The Independent*. Retrieved December 1, 2024 from https://www.independent.co.uk/voices/metoo-disability-women-groped-touched-consent-abuse-a9079016.html

Mason-Bish, H. (2024). 'Every day is filled with unexpected violations'—Examining the continuum of disability hate crime for disabled women. In L. Burch, & D. Wilkin (Eds.), *Disability hate crime: Perspectives for change*. Routledge.

McCarthy, M. (2017). 'What kind of abuse is him spitting in my food?': Reflections on the similarities between disability hate crime, so-called 'mate' crime and domestic violence against women with intellectual disabilities. *Disability & Society, 32*(4), 595–600. https://doi.org/10.1080/09687599.2017.1301854

McClimens, A., Partridge, N., & Sexton, E. (2014). How do people with learning disability experience the city centre? A Sheffield case study. *Health and Place, 28*, 14–21.

Mintz, S. (2007). *Unruly bodies: Life writing by women with disabilities*. University of North Carolina Press.

Mohamed, K., & Shefer, T. (2015). Gendering disability and disabling gender: Critical reflections on intersections of gender and disability. *Agenda, 29*(2), 2–13. https://doi.org/10.1080/10130950.2015.1055878

More, R. (2023). Storying ableism: Proposing a feminist intersectional approach to linking theory and digital activism. *Feminist Theory, 25*(3), 322–337. https://doi.org/10.1177/14647001231173242

More, R. (2024). The relevance of ableism in social (work) pedagogy. *Pedagogy, Culture & Society*, 1–18. https://doi.org/10.1080/14681366.2024.2322738

Morris, J. (1989). *Able lives: Women's experience of paralysis*. The Women's Press.

Morris J. (1991). *Pride against prejudice: Transforming attitudes to disability*. The Women's Press.

Morris, J. (1992). Personal and political: A feminist perspective on researching physical disability. *Disability, Handicap & Society, 7*, 157–166.

Morris, J. (1993). Feminism and disability. *Feminist Review, 43*(1), 57–70. https://doi.org/10.1057/fr.1993.4

Morris, J. (1996). *Encounters with strangers: Feminism and disability*. The Women's Press.

Nario-Redmond, M. R., Kemerling, A. A., & Silverman, A. (2019). Hostile, benevolent, and ambivalent ableism: Contemporary manifestations. *Journal of Social Issues, 75*, 726–756. https://doi.org/10.1111/josi.12337

Nixon, J. (2009). Domestic violence and women with disabilities: Locating the issue on the periphery of social movements. *Disability & Society, 24*(1), 77–89. https://doi.org/10.1080/09687590802535709

Office for National Statistics. (2021). *Sexual offences victim characteristics, England and Wales: Year ending March 2021.* Retrieved October 10, 2024 from https://www.ons.gov.uk/peoplepopulationandcommunity/crimeandj ustice/articles/sexualoffencesvictimcharacteristicsenglandandwales/march2 020#disability

Oliver, M. (1983). *Social work with disabled people.* Macmillan.

Oliver, M. (1990). *The politics of disablement.* Macmillan.

Oliver, M., & Barnes, C. (2012). *The new politics of disablement.* Palgrave.

Palacios, M. (2020, February 19). *Why disabled women haven't joined the me too movement.* Retrieved October 10, 2024, from https://www.audacitymaga zine.com/why-disabled-women-havent-joined-the-me-too-movement/

Papadimitriou, C. (2008a). 'It was hard but you did it': The co-production of 'work' in a clinical setting among spinal cord injured adults and their physical therapists. *Disability and Rehabilitation, 30*(5), 365–374.

Papadimitriou, C. (2008b). Becoming en-wheeled: The situated accomplishment of re-embodiment as a wheelchair user after spinal cord injury. *Disability & Society, 23*(7), 691–704. https://doi.org/10.1080/09687590802469420

Paterson, K., & Hughes, B. (1999). Disability studies and phenomenology: The carnal politics of everyday life. *Disability & Society, 14*(5), 597–610.

Phipps, A. (2016). *Responsible self-promotion: Negotiating the relationships between self and other, myself and 'my' work* [Online]. Retrieved October 10, 2024 from https://phipps.space/2016/02/18/responsible-self-promotion/

Phipps, A. (2020). *Me, not you: The trouble with mainstream feminism.* Manchester University Press.

Porcelli, P., Ungar, M., Liebenberg, L., & Trepanier, N. (2014). (Micro)mobility, disability and resilience: Exploring well-being amongst youth with physical disabilities. *Disability & Society, 29,* 863–876. https://doi.org/10.1080/096 87599.2014.902360

Pring, J. (2003). *Silent victims: The continuing failure to protect society's most vulnerable: The Longcare Scandal.* Gibson Square.

Public Health England. (2015). *Disability and domestic abuse: Risk, impacts and response.* Crown. Retrieved October 10, 2024 from https://assets.pub lishing.service.gov.uk/media/5a806673ed915d74e622e3c8/Disability_and_ domestic_abuse_topic_overview_FINAL.pdf.

Quarmby, K. (2011). *Scapegoat: Why we are failing disabled people.* Portobello.

Reeve, D. (2006). Towards a psychology of disability: The emotional effects of living in a disabling society. In D. Goodley, & R. Lawthom (Eds.), *Disability and psychology: Critical introductions and reflections* (pp. 94–107). Palgrave.

Reeve, D. (2012). Psycho-emotional disablism: The missing link? In N. Watson, A. Roulstone & C. Thomas (Eds.), *Routledge handbook of disability studies* (1st ed., pp. 78–92). Routledge.

Ridgway, P., Simpson, A., Wittman, F. D., & Wheeler, G. (1994). Homemaking and the community building: Notes on empowerment and place. *Journal of Mental Health Administration, 21*(4), 407–418.

Roberts, C. (1989). *Women and rape*. New York University Press.

Rohrer, J. (2005). Toward a full-inclusion feminism: A feminist deployment of disability analysis. *Feminist Studies, 31*(1), 34–63.

RNIB. (2020). *How the lockdown is affecting blind and partially sighted people* (RNIB Briefing Paper). Retrieved October 10, 2024 from https://www.rnib.org.uk/living-with-sight-loss/independent-living/the-effect-of-lockdown-and-social-distancing/

Roulstone, A., & Mason-Bish, H. (Eds.). (2013). *Disability, hate crime and violence*. Routledge.

Roulstone, A., & Sadique, K. (2013). Vulnerable to misinterpretation: disabled people, 'vulnerability' and the fight for legal recognition. In A. Roulstone, & H. Mason-Bish (Eds.), *Disability, hate crime and violence* (pp. 25–29). Routledge.

Ryan, F. (2019). *Crippled: Austerity and the demonization of disabled people*. Verso Books.

Santos, A. C., & Santos, A. L. (2018). Yes, we fuck! Challenging the misfit sexual body through disabled women's narratives. *Sexualities, 21*(3), 303–318. https://doi.org/10.1177/1363460716688680

Saunders, C. L., et al. (2023). Demographic characteristics, long-term health conditions, and healthcare experiences of 6,333 trans and non-binary adults in England: Nationally representative evidence from the 2021 GP Patient Survey. *British Medical Journal Open*. https://doi.org/10.1136/bmjopen-2022-068099

Saxton, M., Curry, M., Powers, L. E., Maley, S., Eckels, K., & Gross, J. (2001). 'Bring my scooter so I can leave you': A study of disabled women handling abuse by personal assistance providers. *Violence against Women, 7*(4), 393–417. https://doi.org/10.1177/1077801012218252

Schalk, S. (2020). Contextualizing black disability and the culture of dissemblance. *Signs, 45*(3), 535–540.

Schein, E. H. (2009). *Helping: How to offer, give, and receive help*. Bennett-Koehler.

Shah, S., Tsitsou, L., & Woodin, S. (2016). Hidden voices: Disabled women's experiences of violence and support over the life course. *Violence Against Women, 22*(10), 1189–1210.

Shakespeare, T. (1994). Cultural representation of disabled people: Dustbins for disavowal? *Disability and Society, 9*(3), 283–299. https://doi.org/10.1080/09687599466780341

Sheldon, A. (1999). Personal and perplexing: Feminist disability politics evaluated. *Disability & Society, 14*(5), 643–657. https://doi.org/10.1080/096 87599925993

Shildrick, M. (1997). *Leaky bodies and boundaries: Feminism, postmodernism and (bio)ethics.* Routledge.

Simplican, S. C. (2017). Feminist disability studies as methodology: Life-writing and the abled/disabled binary. *Feminist Review, 115*(1), 46–60.

Smith, B., & Sparkes, A. C. (2008). Narrative and its potential contribution to disability studies. *Disability & Society, 23*(1), 17–28. https://doi.org/10.1080/09687590701725542

Smith-Johnson, M. (2022). Transgender adults have higher rates of disability than their cisgender counterparts. *Health Affairs, 41*(10), 1470–1476.

Snæfríðar- og Gunnarsdóttir, H., Traustadóttir, R., Einarsdóttir, T., & Rice, J. G. (2023). Through an intersectional lens: Prevalence of violence against disabled women in Iceland. *Violence Against Women*, 1–21. https://doi.org/10.1177/10778012231155174

Stafford, L., Vanik, L., & Bates, L. K. (2022). Disability justice and urban planning. *Planning Theory & Practice, 23*(1), 101–142. https://doi.org/10.1080/14649357.2022.2035545

Stamell, K. (2016, March 29). *People with dwarfism deserve respect—Not ridicule.* Retrieved 10th October, 2024 from https://www.theguardian.com/commentisfree/2016/mar/29/people-dwarfism-deserve-respect

Stanko, E. (2000). "I second that emotion": Reflections on feminism, emotionality, and research on sexual violence. In D. Schwartz (Ed.), *Researching sexual violence against women: Methodological and personal perspectives.* Sage.

Stone, E., & Priestley, M. (1996). Parasites, pawns and partners: Disability research and the role of non-disabled researchers. *The British Journal of Sociology, 47*(4), 699–716. https://doi.org/10.2307/591081

Strike, A. (2018). Disabled women see #MeToo and think: What about Us? *The Guardian* [Online]. Retrieved January 14, 2024 https://www.theguardian.com/commentisfree/2018/mar/08/disabled-people-metoo-womens-movement-inclusion-diversity

Thiara, R., Hague, G., & Mullender, A. (2011). Losing out on both counts: Disabled women and domestic violence. *Disability & Society, 26*(6), 757–771. https://doi.org/10.1080/09687599.2011.602867

Thomas, C. (1999). *Female forms: Experiencing and understanding disability.* Open University Press.

Thomas, C. (2001). Medicine, gender, and disability: Disabled women's health care encounters. *Health Care for Women International, 22*(3), 245–262. https://doi.org/10.1080/073993301300357188

Thomas, C. (2007). *Sociologies of disability and illness. Contested ideas in disability studies and medical sociology.* Palgrave Macmillan.

Thomas, P. (2011). 'Mate crime': Ridicule, hostility and targeted attacks against disabled people. *Disability & Society, 26*(1), 107–111. https://doi.org/10.1080/09687599.2011.532590

Thomas, C. (2019). Times change, but things remain the same. *Disability & Society, 34*(7–8), 1040–1041. https://doi.org/10.1080/09687599.2019.1664074

TUC. (2021). *Sexual harassment of disabled women in the workplace.* Retrieved October 10, 2024 from https://www.tuc.org.uk/sites/default/files/2021-07/DisabledWomenSexual%20harassmentReport.pdf

Vera-Gray, F. (2016b). Men's stranger intrusions: Rethinking street harassment. *Women's Studies International Forum, 58,* 9–17.

Vera-Gray, F. (2017). *Men's intrusion, women's embodiment: A critical analysis of street harassment.* Routledge.

Vera-Gray, F. (2018). *The right amount of panic: How women trade freedom for safety in public.* Policy Press.

Vera-Gray, F., & Kelly, L. (2020). Contested gendered space: Public sexual harassment and women's safety work. *International Journal of Comparative and Applied Criminal Justice, 44*(4), 265–275. https://doi.org/10.1080/01924036.2020.1732435

Tregaskis, C., & Goodley, D. (2005). Disability research by disabled and non-disabled people: Towards a relational methodology of research production. *International Journal of Social Research Methodology, 8*(5), 363–374. https://doi.org/10.1080/13645570500402439

Unsworth, C. A., Rawat, V., Sullivan, J., Tay, R., Naweed, A., & Gudimetla, P. (2019). "I'm very visible but seldom seen": Consumer choice and use of mobility aids on public transport. *Disability Rehabilitation Assistance Technology, 14*(2), 122–132. https://doi.org/10.1080/17483107.2017.1407829

UPIAS. (1976). *Fundamental principles of disability.* Union of the Physically Impaired Against Segregation.

Walters, M. A. (2022). *Criminalising hate: Law as social justice liberalism.* Springer International Publishing AG.

Watermeyer, B., & Swartz, L. (2022). Disability and the problem of lazy intersectionality. *Disability & Society, 38*(2), 362–366. https://doi.org/10.1080/09687599.2022.2130177

Watharow, A., & Wayland, S. (2022). Making qualitative research inclusive: Methodological insights in disability research. *International Journal of Qualitative Methods, 21.* https://doi.org/10.1177/16094069221095316

Wayland, S., Newland, J., Gill-Atkinson, L., Vaughan, C., Emerson, E., & Llewellyn, G. (2020). I had every right to be there: Discriminatory acts towards young people with disabilities on public transport. *Disability & Society, 37*(2), 296–319. https://doi.org/10.1080/09687599.2020.1822784

Webster, L. (2023). *The view from down here: Life as a young disabled woman.* DK Publishing.

Webster, L. (2021). The everyday assault of disabled women: 'It's inappropriate sexual touching at least once a month'. *The Guardian.* Retrieved December 1, 2024 from https://www.theguardian.com/world/2021/nov/25/the-eve ryday-assault-of-disabled-women-its-inappropriate-sexual-touching-at-least-once-a-month

Wendell, S. (1996). *The rejected body. Feminist philosophical reflections on disability.* Routledge.

Whaley, K. (2016, January 26). Nobody catcalls the woman in the wheelchair. *The Establishment.* Retrieved October 10, 2024 from https://theestabl ishment.co/nobody-catcalls-the-woman-in-the-wheelchair-82a6e4517f79/index.html

Wilde, A., & Fish, R. (2024). Gender, feminism and the project of critical disability studies (CDS). *Disability & Society.* https://doi.org/10.1080/096 87599.2023.2298774

Wilkin, D. (2020). *Disability hate crime: Experiences of everyday hostility on public transport.* Palgrave Macmillan.

Wiseman, P. (2019). Lifting the lid: Disabled toilets as sites of belonging and embodied citizenship. *The Sociological Review, 67*(4), 788–806. https://doi.org/10.1177/0038026119854255

Wolbring, G. (2008). The politics of ableism. *Development, 51,* 252–258. https://doi.org/10.1057/dev.2008.17

Wolbring, G. (2012). Expanding ableism: Taking down the ghettoization of impact of disability studies scholars. *Societies, 2*(3), 75–83. Online. https://doi.org/10.3390/soc2030075

Wong, A. (2020). *Disability visibility: First-person stories from the twenty-first century.* Knof-Doubleday.

Wong, S. (2018). Travelling with blindness: A qualitative space-time approach to understanding visual impairment and urban mobility. *Health and Place, 49,* 85–92.

Worth, N. (2013). Visual impairment in the city: Young people's social strategies for independent mobility. *Urban Studies, 50*(3), 574–586. https://doi.org/10.1177/0042098012468898.

Yang, L., & Lin, Z. (2023). The re-imagined social model: the disabling space of disabled people during the pandemic. *Disability & Society*, 1–20. https://doi.org/10.1080/09687599.2023.2295215

Zempi, I., & Smith, J. (Eds.). (2021). *Misogyny as hate crime* (1st ed.). Routledge. https://doi.org/10.4324/9781003023722

Zitzelsberger, H. (2005). (In)visibility: Accounts of embodiment of women with physical disabilities and differences. *Disability & Society*, 20(4), 389–403. https://doi.org/10.1080/09687590500086492

LIST OF DISABILITY ACTIVISTS, CONTENT CREATORS AND EXPERTS

The names listed below are individuals with expertise in disability activism, accessibility and lived experience work.

Amy Kavanagh—Disability rights activist and campaigner @blondehistorian www.amykavanagh.co.uk

Charli Clement—Disability activist, speaker and writer https://www.charliclement.com/

Chloe Tear—Disability writer and activist @chloe_tear www.chloetear.co.uk

Claire Sisk—Blind content creator @canseecantsee

Dr. Amit Patel—Disability rights campaigner and speaker https://www.dramit.uk/

Eleanor Thoe Lisney—Founding Member and Director of Sisters of Frida https://ethoelisney.uk/

Gem Hubbard—Disabled content creator @wheelsnoheels_ www.wheelsnoheels.co.uk

Ginny Butcher—Disabled activist and consultant https://www.ginnybutcher.uk/

Haben Girma—Disability activist, advocate and campaigner https://habengirma.com/

Lucy Edwards—Disability activist and content creator @lucyedwardsofficial www.lucyedwards.com

Lucy May Dawson—Disabled content creator and activist @luuudaw www.luuudaw.co.uk

Jennie Berry—Disability blogger and content creator @wheelie_good_life www.wheeliegoodlife.com

Maria R Palacios—Disability Activist and Blogger https://cripstory.wordpress.com/about/

Nina Tame—Disabled content creator @nina_tame www.ninatame.komi.io

Talila Lewis—Social Justice Engineer (and more) https://www.talilalewis.com/about.html

Journalists/Academics

Becca Jiggens—Disability activist and academic @beccajiggens www.beccajiggens. com/

Frances Ryan—Disability journalist and author @frances.ryan85

Hollie-Anne Brooks—Disabled journalist, content creator and speaker @hollieanneb https://slowlivingwithme.substack.com/

Lucy Webster—Disabled journalist and activist www.lucywebster.substack.com

Melissa K. Parker—Disabled journalist @melissakarenparker1

Prof. Anica Zeyen—Disability researcher and activist https://anicazeyen.blog

Rachel Charlton Dailey—Disabled journalist and activist @rachelcdailey

Books by Disabled Activists and Writers

Clement, C. (2023). *All Tangled Up in Autism and Chronic Illness.A guide to navigating multiple conditions.* Jessica Kingsley Publishers.

Morgan, S. (2023). *Driving forwards: A journey of resilience to empowerment after life-changing injury.* Sphere.

Patel, A. (2021). *Kika and me: How one extraordinary guide dog changed my world.* Pan.

Ryan, F. (2020). *Crippled: Austerity and the demonization of disabled people.* Verso.

Taussig, R. (2021). *Sitting Pretty—The view from my ordinary resilient disabled body.* HarperOne.

Webster, L. (2023). *The view from down here—Life as a young disabled woman.* DK Publishing.

Wong, A. (Ed). (2020). *Disability/visibility: First person stories from the 21st century.* Random House.

Index

The manufacturer's authorised representative in the EU is Springer
Nature Customer Service Centre GmbH, Europaplatz 3, 69115 Heidelberg,
Germany. If you have any concerns regarding our products, please
contact ProductSafety@springernature.com

Printed and bound by CPI Group (UK) Ltd, Croydon, CR0 4YY
24/04/2026
02096369-0001